Dedication

To the memory of my late grandmother, Margaret Kiely.

Acknowledgements

I interviewed Neil Blaney in May 1993 with a view to writing a biographical profile of Dáil Éireann's longest serving deputy. The idea for this book came after that interview. Neil Blaney declined several requests to grant an interview for this biography.

I am indebted to the many individuals who willingly gave their time to discuss Neil Blaney and his political life. Several interviews were conducted on the basis that I would not name my source. My sincere thanks to the individuals in question and to all the other individuals who are named throughout the book.

Thanks are due to the staff of the National Library of Ireland, Dermot Scott in the European Parliament Offices in Dublin, John Gibson in *The Irish Times* and John Bromley, Editor of the *Donegal Democrat*.

Thanks are also due to Derek Speirs, Jon Carlos and the *Sunday Tribune, Irish Times Photo Library* and the *Donegal Democrat* for the photographs, and to John Mulcahy of *Phoenix* magazine for the cartoon.

I am most grateful to Mairead Mullaney in Eiresearch in RTE who was most helpful and patient.

Thanks to the many friends and family who were supportive while I was writing this book.

I owe a very sincere word of thanks to editor, Deirdre Greenan and to John O'Connor of Blackwater Press for their constant encouragement and support.

Special thanks to Orla.

Contents

— 1 —
Where it all began

Eamon de Valera's split with Sinn Féin came in March 1926. He had led Sinn Féin since his unanimous election as President of the party in 1917. The breaking point was over the issue of Republican TDs taking their seats in Dáil Éireann. De Valera believed that should the Oath of Allegiance to the British Monarch be abolished, then Sinn Féin should enter the Dáil. Delegates to the party's conference, however, voted to continue with this policy of not taking their Dáil seats, no matter what changes were made in relation to the Oath. It was a policy option which de Valera viewed as dooming Sinn Féin to the political wilderness. Thus, defeated by a mere five votes, Eamon de Valera and his followers left to form a new organisation – Fianna Fáil.

On 16 May 1926 the inaugural meeting of this new party took place in the La Scala Theatre in Dublin. The first headquarters of the party was opened in two small rooms, opposite the GPO, at 35 Lower O'Connell Street. Aided by contributions from benevolent supporters, the office was furnished with two tables, a few chairs, a small safe and a typewriter. The task of establishing the Fianna Fáil organisation throughout the country at grassroot level was plotted from this office. Under the chairmanship of Seán Lemass, a small organising committee was formed. It was made up largely of Republican TDs elected in 1923 who were sympathic to Eamon de Valera and had joined the new party. Former Minister Kevin Boland recalls being told that 'a few decrepit old crocks of cars' were purchased to transport men like his father, Gerry Boland; the party's first general secretary, Tommy Mullins and Seán Lemass to the towns and villages of the twenty-six counties. At after-Mass meetings throughout the country, they sought to explain Fianna

Fáil policy and enlist supporters for the new party. They were hoping to put down Fianna Fáil's organisational roots in time for the party to contest the next general election.

The strategy adopted was to approach in each area a sympathetic, well-known and respected veteran Republican who was capable of gathering sufficient votes in the 1927 general election to win a seat for Fianna Fáil. One such republican figure, recruited by Seán Lemass in the constituency of Donegal, was Neal Blaney. The Donegal man's 'republican cv' took some beating. He had fought and been imprisoned in the War of Independence and was later on the anti-Treaty side in the Civil War. Blaney's eldest son, Neil, who was to follow in his father's political footsteps, has a vague recollection of the visit of Lemass. The sight of a motor car was still a novelty at that time. He recalls a man driving up the lane to their farm and asking for his father who was two fields away making hay. A well-built, tall and soldierly man, whom people never failed to notice, Neal Blaney was initially opposed to de Valera's action in leaving Sinn Féin to set up Fianna Fáil. He was, however, won over by Lemass's persuasion and gave his commitment to contest the 1927 general election for Fianna Fáil. By getting this commitment Seán Lemass set in train what is today one of the most durable family dynasties in Irish political life.

Neal Blaney was the second youngest of a family of six. His own father farmed a patch of land in Rossnakill, midway up the Fanad peninsula in the north west of Donegal. To the west of Fanad, with the natural harbour of Lough Swilly as a dividing line, is the large Inishowen peninsula. The long, narrow and meandering Mulroy Bay, which lies to its east, separates Fanad from Rosguill, while to the north lie the seashores of the Atlantic Ocean. Fanad has been to the fore in many of the events in Donegal's history, including the Flight of the Earls and the struggle with landlordism during the time of the Land League. In good weather the view from the hills in the area, looking down over Inishowen, Mulroy Bay and the

Donegal Highlands, is what the tourist guidebooks aptly describe as 'picturesque and breathtaking'. To the visitor this is certainly true; but to those who have to work this land to make a sufficient livelihood, this beauty is not always evident. At the head of Mulroy Bay sits Milford town and twelve miles south is the town of Letterkenny which jostles with Lifford for the title of capital of the county. From the rough northern terrain at the tip of the Fanad peninsula, stretching down through Milford to the more urban environs of Letterkenny Town, this area was to become the Blaney family's personal political territory.

In his early teens, Neal Blaney left school to work on the family farm of about ten acres. Scratching a living from a farm of this size, in such barren surroundings, was difficult and Blaney sought to augment his income by acting as an agent for the New Ireland Assurance Company. While working with New Ireland he became friendly with a fellow employee, Joseph O'Doherty, who was at that time a prominent nationalist in the Donegal area. It was O'Doherty who was instrumental in bringing Blaney into contact with the Sinn Féin movement. After joining, Neal Blaney became involved in organising Sinn Féin locally and this activity made him a well-known figure in the western part of Donegal. In 1917 he established a Sinn Féin cumann in Rossnakill, the first in the Fanad peninsula, while a company of the Irish Volunteers was also set up under his guidance. When O'Doherty was chosen as Sinn Féin's candidate for North Donegal in the 1918 general election, Blaney played a prominent role in O'Doherty's campaign.

Neal Blaney also took an active role in the military campaign of the old IRA in Donegal. From 1920 to 1922 he was the officer in command of the Fanad battalion of the IRA's first Northern Division. His involvement led to his arrest and imprisonment in Dartmoor from where he escaped and returned to Donegal to resume his activities for the republican movement. In the Civil War which followed from the acrimonious Treaty debates in Dáil Éireann, Blaney sided with the anti-Treaty forces of the IRA who were known as the 'Irregulars'. It was a bitter and bloody era in Irish history as families and friends divided for and against the Treaty of Independence.

Blaney's activity on behalf of the Irregular forces brought his family to the attention of the Free State Army. His eldest son, Neil Blaney, recalls being told of several incidents involving the Free State forces. 'I was about two and a drunken Captain of the Free State Army came in, apparently rampaged around the place and then kicked me out of my wicker cot.' He also recalls another incident when the Free State forces raided the family's house in Rossnakill during which his mother 'quickly untied her apron and used it to cover a box of ammunition'. Events such as these were to play a large part in shaping Neil Blaney's political philosophy when he himself commenced his own political career. He would be the first to acknowledge that being born when his father was under sentence of death, being kicked out of his cot by the Free State soldier, along with recollections of the raids on his home are bound to have left their indelible mark.

While fighting on the side of the Irregular forces Neal Blaney attained the rank of vice-officer with the Donegal Number 2 Brigade. He was, however, captured again, although this time by the Free State forces and imprisoned in Drumboe, a temporary jail set up in Co Donegal during the Civil War. The Rossnakill farmer, along with four of his anti-Treaty colleagues, was placed on a death list, as the Free State Government embarked on a policy of nominating prisoners for execution after a member of the pro-Treaty forces was killed. Kevin O'Higgins, who was Minister for Home Affairs in the Cumann na nGaedheal Government, sanctioned seventy-seven executions during the Civil War period, while over 12,000 men were imprisoned, many interned without trial. Four of the men on the list in Drumboe were executed while, thanks to an amnesty in 1923, Neal Blaney was fortunate in having his death sentence commuted to penal servitude for life. He was released from prison in July 1924.

In later years his eldest son, Neil, would rally Fianna Fáil members for his own election campaigns with the catch-cry – 'Remember Drumboe'. A short way outside Letterkenny, beyond Drumboe Wood, a cross was erected in the memory of these men whose crime, like Neal Blaney's, was the possession of arms and ammunition. With his release and the ending of the Civil War, Blaney senior returned to his farm in the Fanad peninsula, his republican pedigree impeccable. It was these republican credentials that attracted the attention of Seán Lemass, as he travelled the highways and by-ways of Donegal in his 'tin-lizzie' motor car, seeking a suitable Fianna Fáil candidate for the constituency at the next election.

With such a solid republican background, it was inevitable that Neal Blaney would gain a Dáil seat. When contesting the 1927 general election, and indeed until his last campaign twenty-one years later, he drew heavily on old Sinn Féin allegiances and a sizeable sympathetic republican electorate. Blaney was a likeable, approachable man whose political career was to be marked by his personal face-to-face manner, a characteristic which differentiated his political style from that of his son who was later to enter political life. Eamon de Valera observed of Neal Blaney that, 'during his membership of the Oireachtas he carried out his Parliamentary duties with zeal and was most attentive to his constituents'. His politics were locally driven; he was a county councillor and TD who spent time in his constituency, serving local needs. Blaney's Dáil record certainly shows him to be a solid constituency TD, with his contributions being made largely in the form of questions to Ministers regarding Donegal related matters. Although he never attained ministerial office, Blaney did play a large part in the organisation of supplies during the Emergency years.

In the period up to 1935, for electoral purposes County Donegal formed one constituency with a total of eight seats. The Rossnakill man took one of these seats in the general election of June 1927, receiving over 5,600 first preference votes and he successfully repeated this electoral outcome at the following four general elections. In 1937, Donegal was divided into two separate constituencies – East Donegal with four seats and West Donegal which became a three seater. Blaney's base was in the eastern end of the county and with almost 52 per cent of the total valid poll, he helped Fianna Fáil take two out of four seats.

Gerry Jones, who was employed in the civil service during the 1940s, knew both father and son. 'The homestead was in fact a bastion of those who were living under the shadow of the Border, who knew what the rift in our society meant.' As a family the Blaneys, according to Jones, 'were so dedicated to the ultimate aim of reunification that it was quite illuminating to be part of'. Jones believes that although father and son were unlike each other in very many ways, Neil Blaney 'learnt a lot from his father'. One of the ways that father and son differed was in social outlook as one of the father's associates told political scientist, Paul Sacks, in 1969 when he was conducting a study of the Blaney organisation. 'When old Neal Blaney met his supporters he usually invited them into a pub for a drink and a chat. He had a handshake for everybody, knew every Tom, Dick and Harry. Young Neil Blaney is a teetotaller. He entertains nobody except on very special occasions. Nor is Harry (Neil's brother) a good mixer, doesn't entertain. The old man got on with people of the Opposition much better than his sons.'

Neil Blaney was educated at St Eunan's College in Letterkenny. He was a boarder and his class photograph still hangs on the wall of the college. Nevertheless, since leaving, Blaney has only returned once and that was in the 1980s. He recalls that the pupils were occasionally allowed into Letterkenny Town to go to the cinema. This rule did not prevent young Blaney from missing any films, as he successfully crept out of the college to go to the pictures on a regular basis. Blaney records with some satisfaction that he returned with equal success and that these nocturnal adventures went unnoticed by the college authorities who, if they had caught him, would have punished him with a beating.

Elections were a family affair in the Blaney household. The 1932 general election, which brought Eamon de Valera and Fianna Fáil to power for the first time, was the first election campaign that Neil Blaney was actively involved in. He was ten years old. He recalls how both his sister, Nancy, and himself got no sleep on the night before polling day. Their time was spent cycling the roads close to their home in Rossnakill, putting up election posters for their father and Fianna Fáil. As they put posters up, however, they were almost immediately torn down by a Cumann na nGaedheal supporter who was following them around. On three occasions Nancy and himself retraced their route, only to discover the posters they had put up lying in shreds on the roadside or in the ditch. The two young children were persistent as Neil Blaney remembers: 'We had the last say because we put them up again in daylight and the enemy didn't want to be seen tearing them down in daylight'.

The local Fianna Fáil Party electoral machine was only thrust into action at election time and remained largely dormant in the periods in-between. This was another area where father and son were to differ. Neil Blaney was to attract great fame for his slick, well-oiled political machine which gained the name of the 'Donegal Mafia'. He recalls the elections of 1954 and 1957 with fond memories as his hold on his seat was strengthened and his organisation, which has stood him well ever since, was put in place. The father's machine was not as organised and certainly not as efficient. Political scientist Paul Sacks was to observe that 'during election campaigns he ranged all over the constituency, competing against colleagues and opposition alike'. Indeed, the fact that he did not consolidate his local electoral base lost Neal Blaney his Dáil seat to a party colleague, in the general election of 1938. Convinced that Fianna Fáil could win three of the four seats in East Donegal, Neal Blaney worked hard to promote the interests of the party's third candidate, Henry McDevitt, who had lost out at the previous election. On polling day, at near twelve noon, a telegram was sent out to all units of the local organisation with the message 'Vote McDevitt, Blaney safe'. It was a cruel political lesson for Neal Blaney as this charity cost him his seat when McDevitt, a gold-medal barrister, was successfully elected.

The period 1938-45 is the only time over the last sixty-six years when a Blaney has not represented Donegal in Dáil Éireann. Father and son have between them fought twenty-four Dáil elections, with only this single defeat in all this time. It was this 'Blaney factor' which contributed so greatly to Fianna Fáil's dominance in the Donegal constituency from 1927 onwards. Ironically, with the departure of Neil Blaney from the party fold in the early 1970s a 'Blaney factor' of a different kind emerged and Fianna Fáil's Donegal dominance was significantly weakened.

This defeat in 1938 was not, however, the end of Neal Blaney's political career as, after a five year spell as a member of the Seanad, he regained his Dáil seat in East Donegal. McDevitt, who took Blaney's seat in 1938, failed to get a proposer for his nomination as candidate at the Fianna Fáil convention to select candidates for the 1943 election. A lesson was certainly learned from the 1938 experience because in the following three elections, 1943, 1945 and his last in 1948, the poll in North Donegal was headed by Neal Blaney.

The 1948 general election brought the first Inter-Party Government to power, thus ending sixteen years of uninterrupted Fianna Fáil rule. Under the same umbrella came together Fine Gael; Clann na Talmhan, a group made up almost exclusively of western farmers; the two groups that were then the Labour movement; Seán MacBride's Clann na Poblachta; and Independent deputies including James Dillon, who was then a disgruntled Fine Gaeler.

Many small farmers and workers were disillusioned with Fianna Fáil, and its policy of internment and execution of IRA members alienated a portion of the party's core vote. Indeed, Neal Blaney was himself unhappy with the harsh treatment of IRA prisoners as he recalled his own days under sentence of death in the 1920s. It was Blaney's unhappiest time in political life and he considered pulling out of politics altogether. In the end he remained loyal to Fianna Fáil and, despite the party's loss of power in 1948, he once again enjoyed electoral success, topping the poll in his Donegal East constituency with almost 2,500 votes to spare over his nearest rival.

His eldest son, who over this period worked outside Donegal for the Irish Tourist Association and then for the Department of Local Government as a temporary civil servant, remembers being called back to assist at these elections as nothing was being left to chance. Neil Blaney's heavy involvement in these election campaigns gave him an opportunity to keep in touch with the local Fianna Fáil organisation and marked him out as the obvious successor to his father, whenever such an occasion arose. Neil Blaney was, however, to be thrust into direct political life a lot sooner than anyone imagined.

The 1948 general election was to be the last for the man from Rossnakill. Following a short illness, Neal Blaney died of cancer in November 1948 at the relatively young age of fifty-six. With de Valera in attendance, he was laid to rest with an IRA guard of honour and firing party at his graveside. In a tribute, the Fianna Fáil leader said of the Donegal East deputy – 'Of a quiet, kind and courteous disposition, he endeared himself to members of all parties and was held in high esteem'. He also noted Blaney's proud republican background and how 'throughout the fight for Independence he rendered sterling service to his country'.

The headline of an obituary article in *The Donegal Democrat* in November 1948 very accurately summed up his public life – 'Soldier and Politician'. The sentiments expressed in a memorial verse of poetry, published in the same newspaper, illustrated the extent to which Blaney's nationalist background was respected in

Donegal. Dedicated to 'an old friend, fearless soldier and true patriot', the author Seamus O'Donnell, wrote how:

> *In the fight for our freedom*
> *he stood with the brave,*
> *And long will his name*
> *here be cherished,*
> *And his memory stay green,*
> *as the grass o'er his Grave*
> *when the faithless and cold*
> *shall have perished.*

— 2 —

Enter Deputy Neil Blaney

The death of Neal Blaney opened the way for his eldest son and namesake to commence a political career that today makes him the longest serving member of Dáil Éireann. Seán Lemass, the man who had coaxed his father into political life in the 1920s, chaired the Fianna Fáil selection convention which unanimously chose Neil Blaney as the party's standard bearer for the Donegal East by-election. The date for the by-election had been set for 7 December 1948. By all accounts this convention, held in Letterkenny, was one of the largest the constituency has ever seen. In accepting the nomination Blaney told the convention that, while he had no ambition for political honours, he had yielded to the many and urgent requests from all over the constituency to carry on where his father had left off. In an interview some years later he said, 'If I hadn't been a politician, I would have been an architect or an engineer. I didn't even want to be a politician. My father asked me to take over his seat the day before he died'.

The by-election had assumed a certain importance as it was the first electoral contest since Costello's Inter-Party Government had taken power in the spring of that same year. At the selection convention in Letterkenny, Seán Lemass emphasised this point when he told delegates that, 'It is here in East Donegal that the issue of the present Government's claim to a mandate will be put to the test'. With the late deputy's son as their candidate, Fianna Fáil was favourite to take the vacant seat. Nevertheless, there was no complacency within the party which had been in a despondent condition since the general election defeat earlier that year had put it into Opposition for the first time in sixteen years. The Fianna Fáil National Executive agreed to cover the cost of election address envelopes, expenses for members travelling to campaign in Donegal and the sum of £300 towards the local constituency organisation's election fund.

Two of the parties in Government, Fine Gael and Clann na Poblachta, also contested the election, and the rivalry was such that Donegal East was home to many high profile members from all parties in the week prior to polling day. Eamon de Valera visited the constituency, as did General Richard Mulcahy of Fine Gael and Clann na Poblachta's Seán Mac Bride. The election was intensely fought. The eve-of-poll rallies of Fianna Fáil and Fine Gael were held within fifty yards of each other. It was fair-day in Kerrykeel and Blaney recalls, 'Our meeting started at twelve o'clock and finished sometime after six. I think we beat the others out of it not so much by having more personnel to speak but because we had better amplification'.

The then Minister for Health, Dr Noel Browne of Clann na Poblachta, recalls in his autobiography the 'long, dangerous and stressful drive . . . all the way from Dublin to the top-most point in Donegal' to campaign in the by-election. He remembers 'a hard weekend of chapel gate meetings' before returning to Dublin in the winter rain. Yet, despite the best efforts of Browne and his colleagues, the people of East Donegal stayed true to the Blaney name – returning twenty-six year old Neil Blaney for Fianna Fáil with over 55 per cent of the total valid poll. One local newspaper estimated that, between the three main parties, there were almost six hundred cars from all over Ireland operating in the constituency on polling day, bringing voters to and from polling stations.

Ireland was in many mays witnessing the last of the style of election campaigning which returned Neil Blaney to Dáil Éireann in December 1948. Elections were fought out at after-Mass meetings and rallies. Television was non-existent in Ireland and Radio Éireann, at that time, stayed totally clear of political coverage. The 1965 general election was the first to which television and radio contributed political commentry for the electorate. The transfer of control of RTE from the direct responsibility of the Minister to a semi-State body took the service out of the civil service domain. This freed it to cover political events. Blaney was probably the master of amalgamating the old-style campaign with the tenets of modern media. This ability earned him the respect of his party colleagues and the title of the 'Great Organiser'. Indeed, even today, there are many in Fianna Fáil who talk in revered tones about Blaney's organisational ability.

Neil Blaney speaks fondly of the old-style Irish electioneering which, although still practised in some parts of the country, is a dying trade. 'Meetings brought the politicians much closer to their electorate than does talking at them through newspaper advertisements and radio and TV. As a result, people had more involvement and knowledge of what was going on than they have now.' Rival meetings and rallies often took place within close proximity of each other and insults were deliberately spoken loud enough to provoke the other side. Tempers often exploded as Blaney recalls, 'You could scarcely have a public meeting in those days that you wouldn't have fisticuffs in the audience'.

The East Donegal by-election success was welcomed in Fianna Fáil; the party's National Executive recorded its appreciation to those involved and also to those car owners and speakers who helped in the campaign. The Honorary Secretary's Report, which was presented at the following Ard-Fheis, spoke of the 'outstanding event' of the election of 'Neil Og Blaney' and expressed thanks to all those who had helped out 'particularly to those in Derry City, Tyrone and Fermanagh'. Tributes were paid by all involved to Senator Fred Hawkins who was Blaney's Director of Elections.

Fianna Fáil seized upon the result to taunt the Inter-Party Government, with the National Executive unanimously passing a motion which called on 'the Taoiseach to dissolve the Dáil in order to give the country an opportunity at a general election to confirm the Donegal verdict'. At all subsequent elections up to and including the 1969 general election, Blaney was to head the poll in this constituency on a Fianna Fáil ticket. Despite his departure from Fianna Fáil in 1971, the electorate of what is now Donegal North East remained loyal to Neil Blaney, returning him safely to Dáil Éireann at all elections since then. If the 1948 by-election is included, then Neil Blaney has, in total, fought fifteen successful Dáil elections over a forty-five year period. Today, Blaney holds the distinction of being called the 'Father of the Dáil' as he is the longest serving member, having held this distinction since the death of Fine Gael's Oliver J. Flanagan.

With Fianna Fáil out of government, Neil Blaney took his place on the Opposition benches behind party leader Eamon de Valera and other celebrated Fianna Fáil figures such as Seán Lemass and Frank Aiken. He had celebrated his twenty-sixth birthday the previous October. There were very few other deputies of his generation; he was surrounded in the Dáil by veterans of the Civil War, men who had founded the Irish State. Reflecting on this time, Blaney says – 'It was an amazing time to come in. There were very few people of my own vintage there, but, when I look back now, I realise that that period was the beginning of the first change from the foundation of the State'.

He was introduced to the Dáil just before eleven o'clock on the morning of 10 December 1948 by Eamon Kissane from North Kerry, a former Minister for Defence, who was a republican veteran of the War of Independence and Civil War. With the Oireachtas going into its Christmas recess, it was to be early in 1949 before Blaney got an opportunity to make his first contribution in the Dáil chamber. It was in the form of a query to the Minister for Industry and Commerce, regarding the differential shipping freight rates for coal being applied from Scottish ports to Derry and Buncrana. It was an appropriate enough start, a local Donegal issue that straddled the Border. Indeed, throughout his political career the twin issues of the economic advancement for the North East and, what he perceives as, the political and economic lunacy of partition have dominated Neil Blaney's agenda. 'To Blaney, Donegal is

Ireland and Ireland is Donegal, and the further he goes from the North East the less his interest becomes,' so observes a former colleague of Neil Blaney's, citing this as one of Blaney's major weaknesses and why, in later years, he would resist all attempts to get him to launch a national political party.

Although he was politically inexperienced, Blaney had been weaned on politics and it was not long before he was noticed within Fianna Fáil circles as a man on the move. The new Donegal deputy quickly showed himself to be an effective public speaker, while from the beginning he identified himself with the republican views for which his father had almost given his life. It was during that time in 1922 when his father was awaiting execution that Neil Blaney was born. Subconsciously, this fact left its impact on Neil Blaney. 'Though not, obviously, on a conscious level at the time, I would say that it had a great deal to do with who I am and what I became,' he later told one interviewer. Throughout his political career Neil Blaney has remained loyal to his father's views on the partitioning of Ireland. To some these views make Blaney a political dinosaur, although even those most strongly critical of his political outlook admire his consistency. 'Blaney has remained genuine, committed and consistent in his republicanism over all these years,' Bruce Arnold argues. A former colleague in Dáil Éireann, however, feels that Blaney's failure to stretch his republicanism beyond the partition issue has detracted from his convictions and left them open to dismissal as 'simply more Blaney rhetoric'.

It was to be a relatively short-lived stay on the Opposition benches as Fianna Fáil returned to power following the general election called in 1951, after the Inter-Party Government collapsed. The divisiveness of the groupings that made up the Inter-Party Government contributed to its demise, although the controversy over Dr Noel Browne's 'Mother and Child Scheme' played a pivotal part in the break-up. Fianna Fáil in the 1951 general election only gained one additional seat over their 1948 outcome but, with the Opposition parties unable to agree among themselves, de Valera was able to secure sufficient support from among the fourteen Independents to get the majority needed to return to office.

There was much speculation that Blaney would be appointed Parliamentary Secretary at the Office of Public Works but this was ultimately to prove unfounded. Eamon de Valera called Blaney aside, complimented him on his Dáil performance, but told the Donegal deputy that he would have to bide his time. Blaney was naturally disappointed – 'I had headed the poll, I was on the officer board of the party, but I was too young for Government office. I then had to make a choice whether to continue in politics at all, for in those days a young deputy also needed a full-time job to keep above the poverty line'. Blaney was the eldest son of a family of eleven children which, after his father's death, made him the breadwinner of the family. He had recently given up his position as Organiser with the Irish National Vintners and Grocers Association to concentrate on a full-time political career. He says that he never expected ministerial office in 1951, but after his meeting with de Valera he felt disappointed and it left a bad taste that remained for some time. He says – 'Dev wanted to encourage me but he almost made me give up politics'.

As well as winning his late father's Dáil seat, Neil Blaney was also co-opted onto Donegal County Council to fill the vacancy resulting from his father's death. He was a member of the Council and other associated bodies until 1957. He held the position of Council Chairperson between 1955 and 1957. It was over this period that the infamous and much talked of 'Blaney machine' was established. In his father's time as a public representative, the party organisation was loosely based, between elections, on infrequent cumainn meetings. Neal Blaney senior was a local politician who spent a considerable amount of his time in his constituency, always readily available to meet constituents on a face-to-face basis. When his son was elected, however, the party organisation in Donegal East underwent considerable change. The number of cumainn in the Milford area was increased, making Neil Blaney the leader of the largest single group within the constituency organisation. This position gave him great control over the local party organisation and according to a reliable Donegal source 'the Blaney influence in Donegal politics was increased, through political patronage. Blaney's people got the best jobs'. All these elements helped to strengthen Blaney's electoral base and made it almost impossible for any rival to challenge his position within the party. It was this skill and style with which he ran his constituency organisation that earned Blaney his first national position within Fianna Fáil as a member, and later chairperson, of the organising committee of the party's National Executive.

Unlike his father, Neil Blaney was to be a national politician, away from his electoral base for a large amount of time. He, therefore, delegated many constituency responsibilities to trusted cumainn secretaries and local Fianna Fáil County Councillors. They acted as Blaney's representatives in their individual areas, ensuring that even when the deputy was absent from the constituency his presence was noted and he was kept informed of all relevant matters on the ground. Members of the electorate who wished to meet Neil Blaney were referred, more often than not, in the first instance, to one of his representatives. If the request or problem was serious enough they got to meet Blaney himself. These additional functions gave the local organisation non-electoral responsibilities, which they had not held previously, and served to strengthen the constituency's Fianna Fáil machine, keeping it ticking over until it went into full power at election times. Blaney's dominance over the local party organisation was helped to some extent by the election in 1951 of National School teacher, Liam Cunningham, who was prepared to play a minor role to Blaney within the East Donegal constituency. Cunningham, whose electoral base was in Buncrana, was returned with the aid of Blaney's transfers at each election up to his death in 1976.

When Blaney was appointed Minister for Local Government he relinquished his county council seat and his younger brother, Harry, was co-opted in his place. Harry Blaney is still a member of Donegal County Council today, having been returned for the Milford area at all local elections up to and including the most recent in June 1991. Throughout this period since 1957, he has acted as his brother's principal personal representative in the constituency.

Over time, Neil Blaney's grip over his constituency machine grew to such dominance that he was in a position to travel to other constituencies to assist Fianna Fáil colleagues in their own campaigns. Operating with great efficiency, Blaney and great gangs of his relatives and close local associates descended generally on constituencies where there was a marginal Fianna Fáil seat. Blaney became the master of the by-election campaign and, according to Dick Walsh of *The Irish Times,* he 'was given credit for pulling the chestnuts out of many a by-election fire'. Several Dáil careers, including those of Dessie O'Malley and Gerry Collins, began with a by-election victory which was successfully orchestrated by Blaney. It was this dogged and ruthless determination, not to mention great style and boundless energy, which Blaney and his dedicated travelling supporters brought to these elections that earned them the epithet of the 'Donegal Mafia'. The term was later extended to describe Blaney's Fianna Fáil organisation in Donegal North East which the American academic, Paul Sacks, spent almost a year and a half studying in Donegal in the late 1960s.

The Fianna Fáil Government which was returned to power in 1951 was in a minority position, dependent on the votes of Independents. It was, therefore, inevitable that its tenure would be short-lived, so it came as no great surprise when a general election was called in 1954. The outcome of this election, which saw Fianna Fáil achieving its worst electoral showing since 1932, was the formation of a second Inter-Party Government, once again under the leadership of John A. Costello. Fine Gael won an additional ten seats in the 1954 general election and formed a Government with Labour and Clann na Talmhan. Costello's Government was still, however, short of a majority and had to rely on the votes of three

Clann na Poblachta TDs who, while offering their support, refused to join the Cabinet.

Although disappointed at not receiving ministerial promotion in 1951, Neil Blaney was coming increasingly to prominence as a new generation of Fianna Fáil TDs began entering Dáil Éireann. When the party went into opposition in 1954 Seán Lemass, assuming the title of Director of Organisation, took responsibility for rejuvenating all aspects of Fianna Fáil's structures. It was generally felt that the Fianna Fáil machine had become weakened over the sixteen years in government since 1932, and that the poor electoral results in successive elections since 1948 were directly attributable to this weakened party organisation. In a sense, Seán Lemass was re-doing the work that he had spearheaded after the party was founded in 1926. Brian Lenihan, who was a member of the team that Lemass put together, says that, 'Lemass surrounded himself with younger people who had the energy to do what he saw needed to be done'. Lenihan also recalls seeing a lot of Neil Blaney at that time, and that 'Blaney's organisational abilities were recognised by Lemass'. Blaney's growing stature within the national ranks of Fianna Fáil was evident with his promotion in 1956 to one of the party's Joint National Trustees. He was gradually being rewarded by Eamon de Valera for, as he says himself, 'waiting in the long grass'. Blaney remembers de Valera with fondness – 'Dev talked to all his deputies, individually and in private, at least once or twice a year. He would chat to them for ten, fifteen or twenty minutes, just to encourage them or in some cases to urge them to mend their ways'.

The second inter-party administration fared no better in government than either of its two immediate predecessors. Thousands were leaving the land to face the stark reality of emigration, as the Irish industrial base was not providing near enough jobs to cater for the country's workforce. Between 1946 and 1961 the numbers working in agriculture fell by over one third, the fastest decline ever recorded, with the bulk of this decline occurring on small farms. It was a depressing time economically with emigration averaging at around 40,000 annually, while during the 1950s the numbers in employment actually dropped. This economic paralysis, coupled with a revival of IRA activities, was too much for Costello's Government and when Clann na Poblachta moved a vote of no confidence in early 1957, the second Inter-Party Government fell.

At the selection convention for East Donegal, Neil Blaney told the three hundred delegates present in Letterkenny that, 'If strong Government is not returned to power, we will continue to slide down the slippery slope and land in complete chaos and national bankruptcy'. Although only thirty-four years of age, Neil Blaney was, by this stage, totally in control of the local Fianna Fáil organisation. Previously, it had been Fianna Fáil policy to run three candidates in the four seat East Donegal constituency. In 1957, despite the reservations of some local party members and against the wishes of the Fianna Fáil National Executive of which he was a member, Neil Blaney was in such control of the local organisation that, on his instruction, only two candidates were selected to contest the election. Both himself and Liam Cunningham were unanimously selected as the party's two candidates for the constituency. At all subsequent general elections, the Fianna Fáil ticket in the constituency was Blaney and Cunningham. The geographical spread suited Blaney and, given his control of votes in the local organisation, any attempt to threaten this position was easily nullified.

Those who had fought with his father in the republican movement were among Blaney's strongest supporters; he was after all one of their own. In his acceptance speech at the 1957 selection convention, he emphasised the elements that combined to make Fianna Fáil the party that, at that time, very much saw itself as the great national movement. 'We have both age, wisdom and youth in our party – we have more farmers than the Farmers' Party in the Dáil; we have more labour members than the two Labour Parties have representatives in the country; and as far as republicans are concerned – every member of Fianna Fáil is and ever was and ever will be a Republican.' His audience in Letterkenny that night certainly agreed with Blaney's sentiments as they took to their feet with deafening applause.

Kevin Boland, who was at that time a member of the party's National Executive, recalls being at similar meetings which took place over the following decade. More often than not, at the top of a packed hall, Blaney would be standing on a chair and 'almost like Christy Moore with the sweat rolling off him', according to Boland. 'There were meetings timed for eight o'clock and they'd still be there waiting patiently at 10.30 p.m. when Blaney would arrive. No matter what time he started he'd speak for over an hour.' Boland laughs when he says that if you were to write down any of those speeches, in terms of what Blaney was saying, then they 'probably wouldn't make a word of sense. You wouldn't know where sentences started not to mind stopped, but he held his audience and the speeches sounded good'.

Gerry Jones was a close associate of Neil Blaney throughout the period from the mid-1950s onwards, having become friendly with Blaney through his membership of the Fianna Fáil National Executive. Jones says that Blaney, more often than not, would use a prepared script as the skeleton from which he would develop his thoughts and he would deviate from it as he thought necessary. He recalls one particular night at a by-election rally, when Blaney had a crowd of several hundred people eating out of the palms of his hands. 'I was sitting in the pub very near the platform and Blaney stood up to speak. Now I had heard this type of speech before, an awful lot of what was in it I had heard before, and suddenly I left down my drink and I started clapping and I had sore hands before he was finished. I was listening to a speech I had heard time and time again but still he could introduce a new vigour, almost as if he could capture a nuance that was missing another time, or circumstanes demanded that it would be said in a different way. He was brilliant.' Jones also remembers another fiery speech made by

Blaney, who held what looked like his script in front of him throughout. When Blaney was finished speaking he went to move through the crowd, leaving the paper on a table at the top of the hall. Jones went to pick up what he thought was a script only to be told by Blaney to leave it, that it was only a sheet of paper on which he had written a tip for a greyhound race down the country earlier that night.

At the general election in 1957 Neil Blaney topped the poll in East Donegal with a surplus of 2,468 votes, of which all but 232 votes transferred directly to his running mate, Liam Cunningham, securing Cunningham's election on the second count. Nationally, Fianna Fáil swept back to power, winning exactly half the seats in the Dáil. Sinn Féin, who had four TDs elected, refused to take their seats, which gave Fianna Fáil an overall majority, sufficient to free it from dependency on any Independent deputies. In what was to be his final term as Taoiseach, Eamon de Valera made a gesture to the new, emerging group of Fianna Fáil politicians, promoting to full ministerial rank Jack Lynch, Kevin Boland and the deputy from Donegal East – Neil Blaney.

— 3 —
Minister Blaney – the great organiser!

Having served his apprenticeship as a formidable, dogged and effective Opposition back-bench deputy, Neil Blaney was finally rewarded by Eamon de Valera with a Cabinet portfolio in 1957. He was his constituency's first Cabinet Minister and Donegal's first Fianna Fáil Minister. *The Donegal Democrat*, welcoming his appointment to the Department of Posts and Telegraphs, said of Blaney – 'A young man robust with enthusiasm, he can be relied upon to pull his weight in the heavy work that lies ahead at Cabinet'. Several brass-bands from both sides of the Border headed a huge torch light procession which led Neil Blaney in his ministerial car through the townlands of his native county. There were scenes of unprecedented enthusiasm in Lifford, Letterkenny and the other towns that the Blaney home-coming motorcade passed through on its way to his home village of Rossnakill. Bonfires blazed on the hill-tops as Blaney supporters lined every yard of the route, cheering on their new Minister. It was the early hours of the morning by the time he finally got to Rossnakill, mid-way up the Fanad peninsula, and yet, even at that late hour, friends, relatives and Fianna Fáilers turned out in large numbers to hear Blaney give his speech of thanks. A ministerial career which was to last for thirteen eventful years had begun.

The Department of Posts and Telegraphs was, at that time, located in the GPO in O'Connell Street in Dublin, and one member of the Fianna Fáil organisation in Donegal remarked on the fact that it was 'significant that the son of a great patriot should be now in charge of the GPO where the first seeds of republicanism were sown in 1916'. Significant or not, Neil Blaney's stay at Posts and Telegraphs was, however, to be a short one. The death of Agriculture

Minister, Seán Moylan, late in 1957, necessitated a minor Cabinet reshuffle which brought Blaney to the Department of Local Government (now retitled 'Environment'). Although in those days seen as a relatively minor portfolio, Blaney's nine month stint as Minister for Posts and Telegraphs was by no means an uneventful one, as he began moves towards the creation of a national television service contrary, as he now admits, to the wishes of some of the most senior civil servants in the Department.

Local Government in 1957 was, according to Blaney, 'a Department graveyard' in which all planning had practically ceased through a lack of money, while morale among the staff was almost non-existent. To this day Blaney still remains the longest serving Minister for Local Government. One of his earliest tasks in Local Government was preparing the groundwork for the first constitutional referendum with regard to changing Ireland's proportional representation (PR) voting system. The scrapping of PR and the introduction of an electoral system similar to that in the United Kingdom was seen as being to Fianna Fáil's advantage because it would tend to distort results in favour of the largest party. Most of the Government's time during the spring and summer of 1959 was dominated by arrangements for the referendum, which was held on the same day as a Presidential election. Eamon de Valera offered himself as a candidate for the Presidency against General Seán MacEoin of Fine Gael. It was hoped that by having the two ballots on the same day, de Valera's personal reputation would carry the PR referendum. In the end, however, Eamon de Valera was elected, while the attempt to replace proportional representation with a 'first-past-the-post' system was narrowly rejected by the electorate. On 23 June 1959, de Valera resigned as Taoiseach and was succeeded by Seán Lemass.

Blaney says he got on well with Seán Lemass who was the party's unanimous choice as successor to Eamon de Valera. He found very little difference in the leadership style of the two men. De Valera, he says, was probably a little more personal, and 'even if he had little to say to you about politics, he would talk to you about your father, your mother, your children and your grandchildren'. Blaney admits that 'de Valera cultivated the personal' and that he himself has attempted to apply this type of approach in his own political life. De Valera's Cabinet meetings were marked by full and long discussion of all matters; everything was argued out at the Cabinet table and everybody had their say. More often than not, Blaney says, this method was used by de Valera to bring those who did not agree with him around to his way of thinking. 'Without hesitation I would say Eamon de Valera is the politician who stands out most in my career,' Blaney admits. A Cabinet colleague, Kevin Boland, who was then Minister for Defence, recalls that Blaney was vocal on a wide range of issues outside his own portfolio. 'Of course he'd fight like a lion for his own departmental stuff,' Boland says of Blaney. Even at the Cabinet table it would seem that Blaney did not forget Donegal and he would not hesitate to defend the interests of his constituency. Kevin Boland recalls that 'myself and Mick Moran used to sit beside each other and when Blaney would be talking about rural Ireland we used to write synonyms for Donegal – rural Ireland, a disadvantaged area and all these kind of things'.

There were seldom discussions with Seán Lemass outside Cabinet and Blaney recalls very few non-Cabinet meetings with him in the time he served as a Minister under Lemass. 'His attitude was, "if you're doing the job, well get on with it; if you're not, well then I'll talk to you".' One of Neil Blaney's few non-Cabinet meetings with Lemass took place in February 1964 to discuss the prospects for Fianna Fáil in the by-election scheduled late in that month, caused by the death of Labour Party leader William Norton. Blaney had visited Kildare and reported back to Lemass his feeling that Fianna Fáil was not going to win the vacant seat. Lemass responded immediately to Blaney's request for complete control over the local organisation for the duration of the by-election. Upon receiving Lemass's approval to do as he thought necessary, Blaney upped to leave the room. As he reached the door Lemass asked his Minister

whom he had yet to tell to go – 'Where are you going?', to which
Neil Blaney enthusiastically replied, 'To Kildare'. The ruthless but
highly motivated and efficient Donegal Mafia was sprung into action
to buffer the work of the local party organisation. Despite having
to face Patrick Norton, the late deputy's son, who was a candidate
for Labour, Blaney's tactics paid off and Fianna Fáil took the seat.
Although he was in Kildare from the time of his meeting with
Lemass until the day of the count, Blaney admits of Terry Boylan,
Fianna Fáil's successful candidate, 'I had never met him before the
morning of the count. I had never met him before'.

In the 1960s, by-elections were a lot more common than they are
today, so much so that people at the time almost specialised in by-
election campaigns. Blaney became famous for his flying squad of
supporters, who would travel from Donegal to whatever part of the
country a by-election was taking place in. 'They tended to come in
and ask what was going on, have you done this, that and the other
thing. If there were springs to be sprung, they would do it,' is how
Dick Walsh of *The Irish Times* remembers the Blaney machine. Kevin
Boland and Neil Blaney became the twin names associated with the
Fianna Fáil by-election campaigns throughout this period, although
it is Blaney who gained the reputation as the one with the great
organisational abilities. Dick Walsh recalls that, 'It was a
characteristic of men like Neil Blaney and Kevin Boland that they
very much stood apart and they didn't have very much to say to the
press at that time. This changed very remarkably after both of them
left Government in 1970 and both became very conscious of the way
in which they were seen by journalists and the newspapers. Both of
them became much more approachable'. Walsh also says that both
Blaney and Boland had 'very fixed views about how things should
be and they worked very hard at getting their views across'.

At no time did either man work as hard as during a by-election
campaign. Gerry Jones says that at the end of each by-election,
when he got into his car to leave for home, he would promise
himself that for the good of his legs, sore from canvassing, that

election would be his last. Jones recalls jokingly telling a friend why Blaney would have no such pain in his legs. 'My only fear is that I will lose the power of my legs because I walk everywhere. Mr Blaney doesn't walk anywhere. He is always carried shoulder high.' Indeed, throughout the 1960s, Blaney was carried shoulder high at by-election victory celebration after by-election victory celebration. Bernard McGlinchey and Gerry Jones were among the small band of associates who were close to Blaney throughout this time. Gerry Jones still speaks of Blaney's organisational ability and methods with great respect. He likens them to modern management techniques. 'What Blaney did when he went down was he looked at the body corporate, he looked for weaknesses. He looked for where surgery was required and that had to be done by twelve o'clock tomorrow – he put deadlines on things.'

More often than not, by-elections were held in twos, either on the same day or within the same week: an example would be the by-elections in Kerry South and Waterford which were held within a few days of each other in December 1966. In such a situation, Blaney and Boland would each take control of one constituency. Kevin Boland, however, says that Blaney would not be content with ensuring that everything in the constituency which he had responsibility over was running smoothly. After canvassing was completed in his own area, Blaney would 'come over to pay us a visit to reassure himself that everything was running smoothly'. These 'semi-official inspections' would occur late in the night and Blaney might have travelled half way around the country to get to wherever Boland was stationed. Then, having reassured himself that all was in order, he would return to his own area of responsibility with another day of canvassing ahead of him.

Kevin Boland also recalls that, 'Blaney had five or six key men and they came down from Donegal and taught the locals the Donegal method and by the time things were hotting up they had them working well. It was quite obvious that Blaney was the controller and he expected everything he told them to do to be done. He really did get that spirit going and within two or three days he'd have the local organisation modelled on his own organisation in Donegal. Unfortunately, this wouldn't hold for a general election because Blaney wouldn't be there.'

At times, during the run in to polling day at these by-elections, almost the entire Fianna Fáil Parliamentary Party would be working in the constituency. Each group of the local organisation which went out canvassing was accompanied by a TD or a Senator. As the Dáil would also be in session, an alarm system was in place to get the TDs back to the Dáil if a vote was called. Despite local protests that certain houses were known 'Fine Gael or Labour houses' Blaney would ensure that, without exception, all houses in the constituency were called to by Fianna Fáil canvassers. According to Boland, 'one thing Blaney really got going was the canvass . . . he ensured that every single house, no matter who or what they were, had to be visited by a Dáil deputy who was accompanied by some of the local organisation, and he got that done to my amazement. Every house, without exception, would be called to.'

The by-election in Limerick East in 1968 which elected Des O'Malley was one of the many by-election victories orchestrated by Blaney. O'Malley, however, says, 'I wasn't really convinced that he was any better an organiser than one of many others . . . but he was much more flamboyant and he shouted and roared an awful lot, whereas others didn't. Now that didn't necessarily mean that things were done any better. A lot of the people who were working on my campaign were quite genuinely frightened of him because of the way he used to roar and shout at them'. Brian Lenihan worked on many of these campaigns with Neil Blaney and he recalls a different perspective of Blaney whom he describes as 'a very energetic man, he knew how to inspire people, how to motivate them, how to mobilise them, how to organise them and how to get them going'.

Blaney's approach and style can be seen differently depending upon how one views his methods. He does not have to ask his supporters and organisation for assistance at election time in

Donegal, they simply respond. They know what has to be done and they get on with the job of doing it. Those who were not prepared to give total effort and commitment were not wanted: 'it's 110 per cent or nothing' in the words of one person who has worked with Blaney on election campaigns. Blaney was also the Director of Elections for the by-election in Limerick West in 1968 at which Gerry Collins was first elected to the Dáil. Collins had first worked with Blaney during his student days when he would travel to help out on by-election campaigns. Later Collins was to be interviewed by Neil Blaney for the position of Assistant General Secretary of Fianna Fáil.

Collins says of Blaney, 'He was very demanding and a hard task master, but he never asked anybody to do anything that he wasn't prepared to do himself. People may have cursed him for being as demanding as he was and no matter how well a thing was done, Neil would always maintain that it could be done better. And if it was a Donegal man who was doin' it – he would do it better! But we allowed for that particular attitude! He was well respected because he was a top-class political organiser and he worked himself to a frazzle, pushed himself to the limits to ensure all those election successes.'

Like so many others, Gerry Collins speaks with a great sense of nostalgia about these by-election campaigns which Neil Blaney spearheaded. Blaney, he says had 'a very rye sense of humour and was always cheerful despite maybe a gruff start, if things were not going as well as what they should be. I remember that he would drink gallons and gallons of tea every day and that he smoked practically constantly'. Gerry Jones is one of the best people to comment on Blaney as an election organiser, having worked on so many of these campaigns himself. 'He always felt that the person to whom he delegated something had the same intensity and the same incisive intellect that he had, and he didn't suffer fools gladly. To me he was the greatest organiser I have ever met.' Blaney himself is aware of his attitude during campaigns. In his own words –'I'm the divil to live with during an election'.

Neil Blaney was retained as Minister for Local Government by Seán Lemass when he became Taoiseach in 1959. Housing policy was high on Blaney's agenda. The appalling housing situation in Dublin led to the decision to construct Ballymun. The development won him the praise of the Town Planning Institute which made him an honorary member in the positive light of 'the largest housing project ever undertaken in Ireland'. Blaney took such a close personal interest in the development that even today he can recall the very locks used for the doors, not to mention the name of the Irish firms which supplied the locks.

Although Neil Blaney readily admits that Ballymun is now a tragedy, he does not believe the concept was wrong. Properly supervised, he maintains, it could have become a showpiece. He was, however, switched from Local Government to Agriculture almost immediately after he had declared Ballymun completed. He regrets the decision to give Dublin Corporation control of the tenanting of the development.

'Ballymun was a prize for people who had looked after their houses elsewhere, who were ready to move up in the world literally. There was to be no question of putting large families on the top floors and old-age pensioners half-way up the skyscraper. The mix was to be carefully applied, according to their circumstances and needs, and I was going to oversee it personally. Then I was moved, Kevin Boland took over and let the Housing Department handle it . . . Everybody was shoved in, regardless, some of them with no prospects, and that's no judgement on them, but they needed help, not to be abandoned out there, which is what happened. There wasn't a single amenity built with it. It was a total contradiction of what I had planned.'

Along with his officials, he was responsible for the introduction of a gigantic programme which would bring piped water to the homes of rural Ireland. This project was inspired from memories of his youth, when the local women had to carry heavy pails of water from the local well to their houses. Blaney also introduced the

Road Traffic Act 1965 which was the first significant piece of road traffic legislation since 1933. It required motorists to take a driving test in cars which were certified as road worthy. In introducing the measures Blaney told the Dáil that 'vehicles and drivers should be properly trained and fully fit'. He established An Foras Forbartha which brought together the best professional and practical experts in the planning area. The possibility of paying rates by instalment, new measures on life saving and regulations for caravan sites were all initiated by him. In his period as Minister for Local Government, Neil Blaney also introduced legislation which extended for the first time the entitlement to vote in Irish local elections to non-Irish citizens.

Chronic emigration and unemployment coupled with stagnant living standards throughout the 1950s had forced politicians and policy makers to look again at how they were running the Irish economy. The *First Programme for Economic Expansion* arose from these economic difficulties and it succeeded in beginning the process of modernising Irish economic and social life. The strategy was to end economic protectionism and stimulate the economy by attracting foreign investment. As part of this new policy Seán Lemass announced, in July 1961, that Ireland would follow the United Kingdom in applying for membership of the European Community. Neil Blaney's Department, like all others, was a hive of activity during this time when the Lemass Government moved Ireland forward with vigour and endless energy. Blaney today says he is sad when he recalls these times in the early 1960s when men like himself, Charles Haughey, Brian Lenihan, Paddy Hillery and Donagh O'Malley had things going so well before, as he sees it, Fianna Fáil began to lose its way. 'It is so sad to think what has become of them all since then – and how much they could have achieved – and how little they actually did.'

This group was the core of the new Fianna Fáil generation which was taking up the mantle from the men who had fought in the War of Independence and Civil War and had led the party since its foundation in 1926. Tim Pat Coogan, *The Irish Press* editor, labelled them 'the Men in the Mohair Suits'. They were bright and brash and full of the confidence which symbolised the Lemass era. They moved in high-brow circles, associating with the rich and the famous in so close a manner that it made many people uncomfortable.

TACA, the Irish for 'support', was established in 1966 to elicit financial support from the business community to fund Fianna Fáil's election activities. For an annual subscription of £100, business people were invited to meetings and dinners at which they had the opportunity to meet with Government Ministers. Some of the biggest names in Irish industry were subscribers to TACA, membership of which was heavily concentrated among those in the construction sector. Blaney was also involved, although he was not one of the figure-heads of the support group; it was Haughey, Lenihan and O'Malley who were the politicians most publicly linked with TACA. 'He was not directly part of the TACA group,' according to Dick Walsh. Although he has an amazing capacity to go without sleep(those who have worked on his election campaigns record this ability), Blaney was, at that time, a non-drinker and would not have been one for the late-night sessions involving a number of his colleagues in some of Dublin's most fashionable locations.

Blaney's strong republican views marked him out as a traditionalist, but within this new Fianna Fáil his association with TACA clearly was a departure from tradition. Dick Walsh notes that 'the second parting with tradition, for Blaney, was in the style of his victory celebrations. Long before anyone else in Irish politics dreamed of such lavish displays, he was leading motorcades across the Donegal countryside . . . Bright ties, dark glasses and open cars, swaying with gum-chewing aides, were vivid reminders of another time, another place: the America of the old populist, Huey Long, Governor of Louisiana'.

Many outside the party viewed TACA as sufficient evidence of the corruption of the ideals which Eamon de Valera's Fianna Fáil stood for. 'The selfless idealism of Easter Week has become the self-seeking degeneracy of TACA,' was the opinion of Mairín de Burca in *The Irish Times* in October 1968. There was also disquiet over TACA within Fianna Fáil itself, although Jack Lynch publicly stated that 'no member of TACA has benefited in any way from membership' of the group. Blaney agrees with Lynch on this point.

At the 1968 Ard-Fheis what was seen as an all too close association between politics and business came in for severe criticism. Neil Blaney spoke in favour of TACA, arguing that it was a means through which those who had been successful in business could contribute to making Fianna Fáil a better party for all its members. As the National Treasurer of the party, he was obviously in a position to see the financial rewards of such a fundraising scheme. Those critics of TACA, Blaney told the delegates, were impeding the further development of Fianna Fáil. One reliable source recalls that 'the majority of delegates came to the Ard-Fheis to vote TACA out of existence, until Blaney came to the microphone and made a very strong speech which turned the audience around'. Dick Walsh in his book, *The Party: Inside Fianna Fáil*, tells of one delegate who said of Blaney's speech – 'By Jasus, he has them in the palm of his hand'. There was agreement, however, for a re-structuring of TACA with a reduction in the membership fee. In addition, its organisation was brought more visibly within the control of the party's National Executive.

When Jack Lynch gained greater control over Fianna Fáil after the Arms Crisis, TACA was allowed to fade away and Senator Des Hanafin, a Lynch supporter, assumed control of fundraising. Blaney has a poor opinion of the fundraising approach adopted from the early 1970s onwards when Hanafin worked out of the Burlington Hotel, behind closed doors, seeking financial donations from the business community. The TACA dinners were open and the guest-lists fairly easy to obtain, Blaney says in defence of TACA. He argues that this transparency was preferable to the behind doors approach for seeking business donations adopted after the winding down of TACA. Indeed, it is this secretive approach which has led directly to the allegations of 'golden circles' in recent times, following alleged abuses in the beef industry and the controversies relating to the Telecom and Greencore affairs. Dick Walsh, however, fundamentally disagrees with Blaney's thesis on TACA and the Burlington fundraising of the 1970s. 'TACA was run behind closed-doors. It was secretive. It was open to some people to say they were there when they weren't and for others to say that they weren't when they were. That kind of thing was rife at that time. It wasn't preferable (to Hanafin) and it was just as bad and certainly I think one led to the other.'

TACA was seen by many critics of Fianna Fáil in the 1960s as the personification of the alleged widespread corruption in Irish political life. There were allegations of abuses in the area of planning for the construction industry. As Minister for Local Government, planning law came under Blaney's brief. Neil Blaney readily admits that there was extensive bribery, although he says he took no part in such activities. 'I could have made at least two million quid between 1963 and 1965 if I had been willing to deal in planning permissions. But my response was "Hump you. Whatever chance you had of getting planning permission, if I can stop you now I will!".' It was Neil Blaney who advised Charlie Haughey on his first property purchase. He says that he has a good knowledge of the source of Haughey's wealth, but Blaney denies that this wealth was accumulated from underhand property deals. 'He didn't make any money on illegal or illicit operations.'

Just two years after succeeding Eamon de Valera, Seán Lemass called a general election, but the outcome of this election, held in October 1961, left Fianna Fáil three seats short of an overall majority. Despite this result, Fianna Fáil formed a minority Government which, although it was defeated on several Dáil votes, led the country for three and a half years. The Government introduced the *Second Programme for Economic Expansion* as Lemass's policy of attracting foreign investment began generating solid economic growth. Blaney claims not to have been very impressed by the cross-Border exchanges which Seán Lemass began with Terence O'Neill, his counterpart in Northern Ireland. Lemass went north of the Border to Stormont in January 1965, a visit which was followed a month later by a return visit by O'Neill to Dublin. These exchanges between the Prime Minister of Northern Ireland and the Taoiseach of the Republic were complemented by visits between individual Ministers of the two Governments.

Neil Blaney was one of the most republican voices in the Lemass Government. Being a Donegal deputy he had direct links with the Six Counties as he travelled into Northern Ireland on his way to and from his constituency. As Blaney's supporters often remark, to get from Dublin to Donegal you go north but still end up in the south. It makes little geographical, not to mind political, sense to them. Blaney was also in contact on a regular basis with many members of the nationalist community in Northern Ireland. This was not unusual for a public representative from a Border county, as nationalists in the North were, at that time, largely unrepresented in their own areas due to Unionist gerrymandering of electoral areas. Blaney's attitude to Northern Ireland was clear and has remained consistent in all his time as a public representative. 'We now know from hindsight that the Treaty of 1922 was not a "stepping-stone" towards Irish unity and peace in this land. It was merely a recipe for further division between Irishmen and for continuing violence. We have now come to the ultimate realisation that total British withdrawal from Ireland is the only solution.'

Despite his reservations concerning the policy line Seán Lemass was adopting towards the Six Counties, Neil Blaney was one of those Ministers who went North. Blaney visited William Craig who was Minister for Home Affairs in O'Neill's Government. 'I went to see Craig,' Blaney later said, as he added dryly – 'He never returned the visit.' While he may not like to be reminded of it today, Blaney was pictured with Craig on the steps of Stormont. When Craig, in the early 1970s, proposed a voluntary Unionist coalition with the SDLP, Ian Paisley, who was opposed to the move, reproduced the photograph to discredit Craig by association with Blaney who, in these post-Arms Crisis years, was a figure not favourably received in Unionist eyes.

On the back of the publicity from the cross-Border talks and sustained economic growth, Seán Lemass called a general election in mid-1965. Fianna Fáil campaigned with the slogan 'Let Lemass Lead On' and won half the seats in the Dáil which was enough to return the party to power. Seán Lemass, did not, however, lead on for too long and, in fact, resigned as Taoiseach and leader of Fianna Fáil in November 1966. It came as a shock to many in Fianna Fáil when Michael Mills of *The Irish Press* broke the story. Nevertheless, when the official announcement of the resignation did come, the Fianna Fáil Parliamentary Party was lined up in support of two candidates who had attained ministerial office under Lemass. It was the first contest for the leadership of Fianna Fáil and neither of the two candidates, Charles Haughey nor George Colley, had the support of the majority of Fianna Fáil deputies. Indeed, many were uncomfortable with the thought of either as leader of the party. Kevin Boland remembers very clearly how Neil Blaney became a candidate for the leadership of Fianna Fáil. 'There was no way that the party wanted a choice between Colley and Haughey, they were not going to have it. I knew from the different groups that came to me that the popular selection for Taoiseach at that time was Jack Lynch . . . but at that time Lynch was not prepared to go.' Haughey had already asked Neil Blaney for his backing in the contest but, according to Kevin Boland, Blaney refused saying, 'No Charlie, you haven't got the background'. It would appear that even then Neil Blaney was dubious about Haughey's republicanism.

Kevin Boland says that eventually there came the point where there was nobody to challenge either Haughey or Colley and with a Colley victory a real possibility, he decided that Blaney had to contest the election. He met with Blaney to discuss the situation and Blaney said to him, 'There's only you or I,' to which Boland says he replied, 'Well, that's you!'. Blaney declared as a candidate for the leadership, with his campaign being orchestrated by Kevin Boland. He could have counted on considerable support among rural deputies, while the support for Colley and Haughey, both Dublin deputies, was concentrated almost exclusively in the capital city. Despite his long standing within the party and his renowned organisational abilities, Neil Blaney would have faced the difficulty that his colleagues might have perceived him as a single issue or two issue candidate. The perception was one of Blaney as the Northern Republican or that perception in combination with the kind of business association which he had. In many ways his biggest problem was that he may not have been perceived as having the appeal of say either Lynch or Haughey. Nevertheless, Kevin Boland firmly believes that 'there would have been an overall victory for Blaney'.

Given his position as Minister for Local Government, Blaney was very well-known by Fianna Fáil County Councillors throughout the country. He was also held in very high regard by the ordinary members of Fianna Fáil. Gerry Collins, who worked in Fianna Fáil headquarters in the late 1960s, recalls that Blaney 'was always available to take up invitations to go to all parts of the country, no matter how far they were from Dublin. This is when the roads were not always great and he had very busy ministerial work, but he was always available to meet the organisation'. One colleague maintains that, 'Blaney was known in every corner of Ireland. The people of the cumainn didn't often see Ministers and the Minister they were seeing more and more was this great speaker, this great motivator; this great man who spoke of the things that their fathers spoke about, that they themselves spoke and fought for. They idolised him. They absolutely idolised him'.

Fianna Fáil appeared deadlocked with a bitter split in its ranks apparent in what would have been a closely won election. Had the contest remained a three man election between Colley, Haughey and Blaney there are, indeed, strong grounds for believing that Neil Terence Columba Blaney would have been elected the third leader of Fianna Fáil, in succession to Eamon de Valera and Seán Lemass, as well as becoming Taoiseach of the Republic of Ireland. Such was the deep distrust and bitter antagonism between Colley and Haughey that had Blaney in the first round of voting kept ahead of either of them, he would more than likely have received the support of the eliminated candidate which would have been sufficient to see him victorious.

Today, Neil Blaney says that his motives in contesting the election were 'tactical' and that he never wanted to be Taoiseach. If 'tactical' can be equated with wielding considerable influence over the eventual outcome and the subsequent development of the party, then, with his support base, Blaney would have been able to achieve such a position. He told one interviewer that the role he would dearly have loved was to have been second-in-command. 'Any leader requires somebody right beside him who does the hatchet job for him. And that person should also be the organisational inspiration for his party, if he's to be successful. That's the role I wished for.'

While Blaney may be honest when he says that he would have been a suitable person to fill the role of second-in-command, there can be no doubt that in contesting the 1966 leadership election Blaney could have been elected Taoiseach. Despite his humility when he says he has never seen himself as Taoiseach, the fact remains that throughout his political career, Neil Blaney has fought all electoral battles to win. He is the only member of the 518 member European Parliament to have won a seat in 1979, lost in 1984 and come back victoriously in 1989. This achievement exemplifies Blaney's political drive and motivation. It would have been most unlike the man not to have entered the 1966 leadership election with anything but winning on his mind.

Blaney was, however, never to be given the opportunity to test at the ballot box his support among his Parliamentary Party colleagues because eventually there emerged a compromise candidate in the form of former GAA star, Jack Lynch. Kevin Boland says that Seán Lemass 'panicked' with Blaney's declaration because 'he knew that there was going to be a fight and . . . that Blaney would win'. In order to avoid this irrecoverable and public split which was emerging, Seán Lemass prompted Jack Lynch as a compromise. A Cork deputy, Lynch had more ministerial experience than the other candidates, but had not even been mentioned previously as a likely candidate in the eyes of the public. Nevertheless, all sides in the 1966 leadership contest openly admit that Lynch was the popular party choice. Blaney and Haughey withdrew, almost automatically, when Lynch declared his candidature. Colley was more hesitant, believing he could still defeat Lynch. Seán Lemass sent for Blaney, who asked the outgoing leader – 'What will George do ?'. According to Blaney, Lemass quipped – 'Jack has got his wife's permission to run, George will have his wife's agreement to withdraw'. Colley did not withdraw, however, and in the ensuing contest he was beaten by Jack Lynch by 51 votes to 19.

Blaney later remarked that he regretted the way the 1966 leadership contest turned out. He readily admits to having played a large part in bringing about the succession of Jack Lynch. 'We were foolishly blinded by the necessity for unity in the party,' he says. 'My experience of him would have been a man who didn't have any conviction about anything.' Neil Blaney, today, is of the opinion that Lynch's assumption of the leadership mantle 'was the beginning and the end of Fianna Fáil'. He finds it difficult to compare Lynch with his two predecessors, mainly because of the Corkman's lack of republican credentials. As Blaney sees it – 'Lynch literally didn't have a Fianna Fáil background at all, it would have been the reverse if anything'.

Despite these reservations, which emerged later, there does appear to have been widespread belief that Lynch was the safest bet as leader, in the interest of party unity. Brian Lenihan echoes this sentiment when he says that, 'there was greater party discipline and sense of loyalty at that stage. Blaney could have pushed it himself but he chose not to, he chose to go for the consensus candidate. We had a much more disciplined party and you could talk to Blaney at that time, which people did, and say, "Look it Neil, Lynch is the sensible candidate, let's get him through without any contest . . . to keep the party going and we'll have a smooth succession." That type of appeal functioned at that time with most people. It did function with Neil Blaney and he withdrew his candidature'.

Neil Blaney says that once Jack Lynch was elected leader, he personally worked as intensely as before for the person who held the position of leader of the party. Blaney's commitment of loyalty may very well be true, but it is fair to say that Blaney, like other Cabinet members, did find it difficult to accept Jack Lynch as leader. They were continuously watching and waiting for him to stumble, while simultaneously watching each other's moves, in the event of the leadership position becoming vacant. Blaney and Boland saw themselves as the torch-carriers of the tradition of Fianna Fáil. Pure, unstained, Fianna Fáil blood ran through their veins. Men like Lynch, who lacked a history with the party or a link to the fight for political freedom in the 1920s, were, in the eyes of Blaney and Boland, only partial Fianna Fáil. Jack Lynch may have been chosen as leader of Fianna Fáil but only after receiving Blaney's and Boland's mark of approval and they still remained the big organisational men within the party who sought to call the shots. Kevin Boland says their backing of Jack Lynch 'wasn't out of any assessment of Lynch, from the point of his suitability or ability at all. I remember distinctly, saying to Blaney, "Look it, let him on so long as he does what we tell him".'

Jack Lynch had assumed the leadership of a political party in a state of transformation. His Government contained no veteran of the de Valera years and he initially had no real die-hard supporters at Cabinet. Blaney and Kevin Boland were two of his fiercest critics and he told one mutual acquaintance that, 'Neil is difficult and Kevin is impossible'. One source claims, however, that Blaney 'totally underestimated Lynch' who, despite his initial uneasiness in the job, was never going to be a Taoiseach on a string pulled by Blaney and Boland. Indeed, this same individual believes that the perception held by Blaney and others that Lynch's tenure as leader was going to be a short one was added to by speculation about his health. This source believes that such talk grew out of an incident, not long after his election as Taoiseach, when Jack Lynch collapsed at a function in Galway. The truth, it would seem, is that the pipe-smoking Lynch, having mislaid his tobacco, borrowed a little from the Archbishop of Tuam. Unfortunately for Lynch the Archbishop's brand of tobacco was different from his own and 'it caused him to turn green almost immediately and collapse'.

Nevertheless, Neil Blaney still insists that he was loyal to Lynch at that time, saying that, 'Organisationally, I worked my heart out to make him an acceptable, credible and successful leader by fighting by-elections beyond and above the call of any person in Fianna Fáil'. Lynch's first electoral test was in Kerry South in December of 1966. 'I worked and sought that victory. We literally stole that election,' is how Blaney recalls the by-election which was Jack Lynch's electoral take-off. Gerry Jones remembers this by-election as one of the great triumphs of the period. He recalls that when Blaney arrived in Killarney, one of his first tasks was to strengthen the local organisation. 'We were going around Killarney making everyone cumainn chairman and secretary . . . and of course fellows were over the moon to be approached.'

One associate remembers Blaney sending Brian Lenihan out to look after the canvass in the Dingle area, where the organisation was thought to be particularly weak. Shortly after Lenihan departed from the election headquarters in Killarney, Blaney said to this man, 'Ring the Europa Hotel and ask for Brian Lenihan'. Blaney's associate looked at him in amazement as he replied, 'But Lenihan's already gone to Dingle'. Asked a second time, but not as politely as the first, the man in question proceeded to ring Killarney's Europa Hotel. Several minutes after asking the receptionist to page Lenihan, what did he hear only Lenihan's voice at the other end of the phone! A short time later, Lenihan was back in the election headquarters where an irate Blaney 'let him have it'. The Dingle vote obviously held up, however, as Fianna Fáil took the seat in

Kerry South. There were four more victorious by-elections to come before Lynch's first general election test.

One of these by-elections was that which elected Desmond O'Malley to the Dáil. He was chosen to stand for Fianna Fáil in the by-election caused by the death of his uncle, Donagh O'Malley, in the spring of 1968. Blaney arrived into the constituency in his usual way, taking over and directing the local organisation. Dick Walsh says that, 'O'Malley felt very resentful at Blaney's coming in and adopting a very aggressive style'. O'Malley himself recalls that Blaney arrived saying that he wasn't altogether happy with the way the campaign was going and therefore he was taking over. The Fine Gael candidate was Jim O'Higgins, a nephew of Kevin O'Higgins who, as the Minister for Justice during the Civil War, had sanctioned the execution of seventy-seven republican prisoners. Fine Gael, O'Malley says, 'went around Limerick rather foolishly, I think, painting in white the name O'Higgins on footpaths. One was conscious of the fact that this name was painted in white in hundreds and hundreds of places all over Limerick'. This action created a certain amount of annoyance but it was nothing compared to the outrage which was to follow.

'One night Blaney organised a group of his people from Donegal to paint the figure 77 in red paint, immediately under or after the name O'Higgins on every one of them that appeared in Limerick.' Blaney was hoping to stir the feelings that remained in Limerick from the Civil War, although whether or not such a policy was suitable to Limerick is debatable. The following morning the red 77s, O'Malley says, 'caused absolute fury and it lost me a lot of potential votes that I might have gotten'. Nevertheless, one senior Fianna Fáil figure who was involved in that campaign maintains that 'if it hadn't been for Neil Blaney's involvement, then Des O'Malley would not have won that seat. O'Malley was an unknown and the party organisation in Limerick City simply did not exist'. *The Limerick Chronicle* observed that 'it should be recorded that this was not a quiet election and was not a clean one. Many should ask themselves if their activities were out of place'. *The Sunday Press* reporting on the by-election used a headline 'Big Guns in Limerick by-election', in reply to which one local retorted, 'It's a pity they didn't use them to shoot down the street painters'. Neil Blaney, however, was only concerned with ensuring victory and, regardless of O'Malley's annoyance, Blaney was content with yet another by-election win.

The bitterness which arose between O'Malley and Blaney in 1968 still lingers. Blaney believes that the Limerick man should never have joined Fianna Fáil, not to mind have been a party TD, while Des O'Malley feels that Blaney 'has a feel for Fianna Fáil in its more primitive aspects but with huge emphasis on its historic roots and genesis rather than on its contemporary or future strategies: this constant harping back to the past and especially to the Civil War which kind of obsessed him, in a sense. Even in private conversation, he'd be making all these allusions and references to things that happened in Donegal during the Civil War. He used to be constantly alluding to the incident at Drumboe. It was one of the things that drove him on'.

The Limerick East by-election in 1968 is famous also for a celebrated incident involving Neil Blaney and Bobby Molley, who was at that time a Fianna Fáil back-bench deputy. A reliable source recalls the incident which took place at a hotel in Limerick at a dance which had been organised after the polling booths closed on the night before counting, for all those who had canvassed for O'Malley.

'Bobby Molloy turned up with a group of people who had been working with him, to bring them to this dance and apparently Blaney was there at the door and he roared at Molloy that they couldn't come in unless they were paid for. So Molloy protested that he thought that it was unreasonable to ask people who had been working hard all day to pay in to the dance. And that apparently led to a rather celebrated incident where Blaney is alleged to have hit Molloy in front of all these people and caused quite a stir. That was indicative of the style of the man, at that time.'

Blaney's associate, Gerry Jones, feels that the relationship between Jack Lynch and Neil Blaney went well until after the referendum defeat in 1968. Fianna Fáil had again proposed the abolition of the proportional representation electoral system and its replacement with a straight vote system. This time, however, the Government was handsomely beaten. 'I think himself and Lynch got on pretty well together until the referendum, that was the turning point for me . . . There was an inquest held in Mr Haughey's house in Grangemore, the house he occupied before he went to Kinsealy, and all the elders of the party were there and I was there as a member of TACA.'

According to Jones a 'good share of wine was consumed' and little talk was given to the referendum defeat. Nevertheless, he did get speaking to Jack Lynch and advised him that a Cabinet re-shuffle may be in order. Jones says that he had two Ministers in mind and was about to name them when Lynch interjected, '"Gerry," he said, "What can you do with Neil and Kevin?" He said, "Kevin has a commitment that frightens me and Blaney has an intellect that I covet," they were his actual words'. In the light of Lynch's outburst to Jones, a meeting was held to determine what action to take. 'Kevin, Neil and I held a special meeting outside, under the stand in the Curragh, on the day of the Derby, so we wouldn't be seen.' Blaney, however, told his two colleagues that he was not going to change his point of view on any issue.

In his first Cabinet Jack Lynch moved Blaney from Local Government to the Department of Agriculture and Fisheries, which had been Charles Haughey's brief in the last Lemass Government. The farmers' organisations had organised a nationwide campaign to highlight the plight of farmers and attempt to stave off any reduction in their political influence, as the new policy of industrialisation was being embarked upon. The National Farmers' Association, in particular, adopted an aggressive lobbying style and during Haughey's time in Agriculture thousands of farmers had descended upon the streets of Dublin to protest against what they saw as a lack of Government commitment to the sector, and they succeeded in occupying the offices of the Department of Agriculture. After he was elected Taoiseach, Jack Lynch, in an attempt to defuse the situation, let it be known that the National Farmers' Association had the right of consultation with his Agriculture Minister 'at all reasonable times'. Neil Blaney did not take kindly to the Taoiseach's intervention and at various stages he turned down meetings the farmers were seeking. Blaney was antagonistic to the political approach adopted by the Farmers' Association which was led by Rickard Deasy. According to Deasy, when Blaney was Minister for Agriculture he would have very little to do with the NFA and voluntary organisations, preferring to deal with 'political farmers'. 'I had a friend in the army who used to say "nothing much doing", and that very much sums up my opinion of the man.'

J.C. Nagle, who was Secretary of the Department of Agriculture from the late 1950s until his retirement in 1972, speaks highly of Blaney. He recalls when Blaney was appointed Minister for Agriculture. 'He was known . . . people had a good idea what he was like as a Minister – a forceable character who didn't mince words. That pleased people, on the whole, I would say. He kept politics out of it although he had strong political views. I must say, to be fair, he never intruded these views on any of the officials.' Nagle identifies Blaney's dealings with the NFA and a scare of foot and mouth disease as the principal issues during his time as Agriculture Minister. 'Both of these problems he handled very well I thought.'

The policy of economic expansion was increasingly putting greater emphasis on industrial development and there was a declining trend in the percentage of Irish exports directly accounted for by agriculture, down from 80 per cent in 1951 to just over 52 per cent in 1966. The sector was heavily dependent upon the British market with almost 80 per cent of Irish agricultural exports going to the UK in 1966. Blaney was Minister for Agriculture while the sector was in a state of transition. The old policies of protection were giving way as policies were being developed with future membership of the European Community in mind. Rickard Deasy was succeeded as President of the Farmers' Association by T.J. Maher, who was later to become a colleague of Blaney's in the European Parliament. Maher believes that the Government and civil service had difficulty coming to terms with the strengthening position of the Farmers' Association. 'Pressure groups were seen as being a nuisance and they believed that we were eventually going to lie down. Ten good years were lost when we should have been preparing for Common Market membership and Neil Blaney must share some of the blame for this.'

A part of the NFA's obstruction policy was at one stage to refuse to hold fairs and marts throughout the country. T.J. Maher recalls that the holding of the fair in Donegal Town became a matter of contention, with Blaney declaring that it would go ahead 'NFA or no NFA'. On the day in question, Maher was in the NFA's headquarters in Dublin when a phone call came through from Donegal. To Maher's delight the NFA organiser in Donegal said, 'It is twelve o'clock in Donegal Town and not a beast in sight, not even a Blaney'.

Nevertheless, Maher does admit that after he became President of the NFA in 1967, tensions between Blaney and the NFA eased off and that 'normal relations were eventually restored'. Jack Nagle recalls that Blaney 'made the NFA understand that he wasn't going to bow to too much pressure of a propaganda kind, so to speak, and I think they understood that. He understood them because he was connected with the land himself. He didn't actually hate them – he understood that they were a pressure group and that they had a job to do . . . Nevertheless he had some very long sessions with them, even when he disagreed. One meeting went on very late at night, if I recall correctly they were beginning to get fed up at the late hour, and I think he said that he was prepared to go on as the matter was so important. He had that tough element in him'.

Nagle also remembers that Blaney 'didn't object to you telling him what one thought . . . he didn't like fustering, that wouldn't please him, but he didn't mind you speaking your piece even if he might strongly disagree. He had fairly strong opinions all right and he had great sympathy with the smaller farmer'. In an attempt to assist smaller farmers Blaney introduced a favourable milk scheme for them while he was Minister for Agriculture, although such tiered pricing was eventually abolished when Ireland joined the EC.

A general election was held in the Republic on 18 June 1969. It was Lynch's first as leader and an important test for a man whom many in Fianna Fáil, including Blaney, considered a stop-gap, interim leader who would fill the post until others were in a position to command sufficient support to take the leadership. Of more immediate concern to Fianna Fáil, going into the 1969 general election, was the possibility of a significant breakthrough by the Labour Party, invigorated by the influx of intellectual heavyweights such as Conor Cruise O'Brien and Justin Keating. Brendan Corish, the Labour Party leader, announced that his party was intent on securing a majority in Dáil Éireann and they put up ninety-nine candidates to fulfil this aim. The Labour Party call that 'the '70s would be socialist' was taken seriously by Blaney and Haughey, who were the organisational masterminds behind the Fianna Fáil campaign. A continual barrage of criticism was thrown at the Labour Party, with Fianna Fáil launching a particularly bitter assault on the so-called 'foreign' element which they claimed had taken hold of the upper legions of the Labour Party. Blaney, in a none too subtle address in the middle of the campaign, claimed that, if put into power, the Labour Party would invite the Soviet Union to establish nuclear bases on the Irish coast.

The reaction which Lynch received in Donegal during his election tour, referred to as 'the tour of the reverend mothers' because of the large number of convents visited, was nowhere near equalled in any other part of the country, including his home county of Cork. The Blaney machine was out in force to buoy up the

Taoiseach and give him a strong confidence injection for the run in to polling day. At a rally in Letterkenny, some 5,000 people gathered to listen to speeches from the Taoiseach and Fianna Fáil's Donegal candidates. Senator Bernard McGlinchey, who was Director of Elections in Donegal North East, told the crowd of how he had met a Fine Gael supporter earlier in the day who had said to him, 'There is one man in Fianna Fáil I absolutely detest and that is Neil Blaney,' to which McGlinchey told the delighted crowd he responded – 'Sure if you loved him he would be no damned good to us'.

Blaney was in his element. According to Andrew Hamilton, writing in *The Irish Times*, 'Neil Blaney came on chewing gum and wearing dark glasses. He gave a super-charged performance of colourful words'. Blaney began by saying that the '1969 election will go down in the books as the election of the hairy half-truth, of the television twisters and the comrades of Cuba'. As he warmed to his speech, Hamilton wrote, 'Neil Blaney's face grew more and more purple'. Blaney rounded on Fine Gael and Labour and warned his audience of 'a rag-bag Coalition that will damage this country's economy overnight'.

Rosguill was to be the final destination of Jack Lynch's Donegal tour and his place of sleep after a long, hard day on the hustings, which took him from Bundoran through towns like Ballyshannon, Ballybofey, Lifford and Moville. The twenty-five mile journey from Letterkenny to Rosguill which, in normal circumstances, would have been a half hour's drive, seeing the Taoiseach in Rosguill at about 11 o'clock, took almost two hours. The Blaney machine was out to impress in style. Every hundred yards of roadside from Letterkenny to Rosguill had a blazing tyre. A huge truck moved ahead of the Taoiseach's motorcade, dropping the tyres and then, almost in military style, Fianna Fáilers jumped from their cars and vans to set fire to the tyres and start a blaze. Blaney's organisation had the bonfires blazing on the Rosguill hillsides and the night-time sky was alight to welcome the Taoiseach. At strategic points along the route there was a bonfire and a cheering crowd gathered. The motorcade was led by a Ford Zephyr with a loudspeaker which added to the atmosphere by blaring out traditional republican songs. The State car with Lynch and Blaney aboard stopped at pubs, crossroads and villages along the way to greet the faithful. It was ironic, particularly so in light of subsequent events, that with a campaign plotted and orchestrated by his internal party rivals, Jack Lynch led Fianna Fáil back into Government in 1969 with a five seat majority.

Although it could be said that in light of the events surrounding the Arms Crisis Neil Blaney's opinion of Jack Lynch has been tainted, the relationship between the two men was in fact never easy. While Northern Ireland policy was an obvious source of tension between Blaney and the new leader of Fianna Fáil, it was not the only area where difficulties arose. T.J. Maher recalls a meeting between the NFA and Blaney which Jack Lynch also attended. 'The friction between Jack Lynch and Neil Blaney was obvious.' Lynch had wanted to move Blaney out of Agriculture and Fisheries after the 1969 general election into a new Department of Planning which he proposed establishing. Blaney resisted such a move and, according to one reliable source, 'he stormed into Lynch's office and banged the table, until that was the end of that'. Blaney was retained in Agriculture and Fisheries.

According to Dick Walsh of *The Irish Times*, Jack Lynch has said that he 'might well have fired Blaney whether he was involved in the 1969-70 arms business or not, because he considered him to be an inefficient Minister. Now, whether that's so or not I just don't know'. Yet, a Cabinet colleague of Blaney's, Brian Lenihan, says that Blaney was 'a very good Minister, in terms that he was able to conduct a huge Department of State, one of the biggest spending Departments. He didn't have any quangos around him to help him, he didn't believe in quangos . . . he didn't believe in surrounding himself with a host of committees or advisors or anything like that. He was a great action political manager and leader; and he ran the

Departments of Local Government and Agriculture in that manner. He was one of the best and most effective Government Ministers we ever had in this country, there's no question about that. And in those two Departments he showed his mettle'. The Secretary of the Department of Agriculture while Blaney was Minister adds that Blaney 'liked to hear about a thing quickly, not too much introduction. He liked to get to the kernel of the problem and he was very good at understanding problems I think. He was quick to make a decision . . . and once it was done it was done; and then he stood by it, which was very good.'

Developments in Northern Ireland in the late 1960s combined to precipitate a crisis which was to rock to the roots the Fianna Fáil Government and Party. In August 1969 there was rioting on an unprecedented scale throughout the Six Counties, particularly in Derry and Belfast, which resulted in the first casualties of the current Northern Troubles. The rioting was sparked off by a provocative Apprentice Boys' parade through the predominantly nationalist city of Derry. It led to a complete breakdown of law and order and ultimately to the intervention of British troops. Lynch's 'we won't stand idly by' speech and his request for United Nations' intervention gave the impression that active involvement by the Republic's army was likely.

For the remainder of 1969 and early 1970 the situation in Northern Ireland was relatively peaceful, with many optimistic that the reform of Local Government which was being rushed through the Stormont Parliament would restore permanent order and stability. It was common knowledge that during the lull in the first few months of 1970, arms for the IRA were coming into Ireland from sympathetic Irish-Americans. It was, however, the events of the first two weeks in May 1970 that were to shock the entire nation. The Taoiseach informed a thunderstruck Dáil that he had dismissed two of his most powerful Ministers for alleged involvement in the illegal importation of arms.

In many ways the divergent opinions held by Lynch on the moderate side and Blaney's more rigid republicanism on the other, reflected the deep-seated tensions which bedevilled the Fianna Fáil Party's attitude to Northern Ireland. Blaney, who described himself as an Ulsterman and a Northerner, was an outspoken Republican in the traditionalist mould who believed that British withdrawal and an end to partition should be the corner-stone of the Republic's policy with regard to Northern Ireland. To the Donegal Minister, such a policy was merely a continuation of de Valera's and Fianna Fáil's historic attitude to the issue. His close contact with groups in Northern Ireland gave him first-hand knowledge of the discrimination which was inflicted upon nationalists in all spheres of socio-economic and political life. This direct awareness of the experiences of the nationalists underlined Blaney's attitude to the Six Counties and while his critics lambasted his 'hard-line' approach, Blaney's response was that only with the removal of partition would the plight of nationalists be ended. The policy line adopted by Lynch was, in Blaney's eyes, mere 'pussy-footing' to the British Government and never going to do anything for Irish citizens in the Six Counties.

The differences on Northern Ireland within Fianna Fáil were never far from the surface. One such occasion when the tension became public was in November 1968 when Blaney, addressing a party meeting in Donegal, launched an attack on Northern Ireland Prime Minister, Terence O'Neill, calling him 'a mere bigoted junta'. Given that Blaney's speech was totally at odds with the Lynch line on the North, it was anticipated that there would be some form of rebuke of the Minister for Agriculture. At a meeting of the party's National Executive three days after Blaney's speech, Lynch adopted a conciliatory approach to his outspoken Minister, concentrating on the need for reform and cross-Border co-operation. Touching on partition and the Blaney line, the Taoiseach noted that the Border continued to arouse 'deep feelings and emotions in people and it is natural that expression will be given to their emotions'.

Blaney was not, however, going to desist from speaking out on the injustices which he saw in Northern Ireland and which he attributed directly to the partitioning of the island and the presence of the United Kingdom in the Six Counties. 'The most democratic election the North has ever had' was what Terence O'Neill called the Northern Ireland general election held in February 1969. Whatever about the democratic merits of the election, Neil Blaney called on nationalists to make reunification central to the campaign, as he urged voters in the Six Counties not to support candidates who were in favour of the Union with the United Kingdom. It was a conflict of views which was eventually going to come to a head and permanently impact upon the political careers of all those involved.

— 4 —

The North, Arms and Confusion

Neil Blaney received a phone call from his sources in the Bogside shortly before midnight on 12 August 1969, detailing the extraordinary events that were taking place in the North. It was not unexpected news to Blaney as he had been preaching about the issues north of the Border for some time, although these speeches were mostly falling upon deaf ears.

'My colleagues weren't aware of what was happening in the Six Counties, even though I was feeding them at every opportunity. Partly because it was the end of the '60s, that period of optimism and idealism – everything was swinging I was told – they didn't want to hear this gobshite from the North telling them about the signs he'd been reading, that were totally at variance with the euphoria at the time.'

Upon receiving the news of the rioting in the North Neil Blaney immediately contacted the Department of Foreign Affairs, but he was unable to get in touch with the Taoiseach. He says that he was up until five o'clock that morning, sitting on the stairs in his Dublin home, trying to contact the Taoiseach, while others, including the Secretary of the Taoiseach's Department, were also attempting to locate Lynch. Blaney feels that the actions the Taoiseach could have taken as a result of the events of 12 August 'should have been Lynch's big moment in history' but says that his experience on the night of the 12 and 13 of August 1969 was that Lynch did not simply just miss leaving his mark on history but that 'he deliberately avoided it'. Blaney recalls that, 'He just could not be got out of his house by the phone or physically during the hours of twelve midnight and five o'clock on the morning of August 13th.' He adds that Lynch's Private Secretary went out to his house at around one o'clock to ascertain whether Lynch was there from the guards who were stationed outside. 'And, yes, he was. He had come in, both Maureen and himself. That poor Secretary went up to the door, knocked on it, rang the bell. He could hear the two phones ringing. He eventually kicked the door. Maureen and Jack were inside and Jack did not emerge.' All efforts to contact Jack Lynch until the morning failed. This leads Blaney to claim that Lynch 'avoided '69 . . . he didn't want to know'.

After the Taoiseach was eventually contacted and briefed, a Cabinet meeting was scheduled for the following morning to discuss the situation in the North. Jack Lynch presented his Ministers with a statement drafted by his civil servants, which he wished to release as the Government's response. It was far from an adequate response as far as Boland and Blaney were concerned and they applied pressure for a hardening of the Government's attitude to the Six Counties and a re-drafting of the statement. Blaney argued for a return to what he believed as the 'true republican ethos' of Fianna Fáil. Lynch was in a minority at Cabinet as the so called 'hardline' stance of Blaney and Boland won sympathetic support from Haughey, Lenihan, Seán Flanagan and Jim Gibbons.

The Cabinet meeting of 13 August requested that the British Government apply immediately to the United Nations for the urgent dispatch of a peace-keeping force to the Six Counties. Significantly, in light of future events, the Irish Army authorities were directed to establish field hospitals in County Donegal, adjacent to Derry, as well as along the Border. Moreover, the British Government was called upon to enter into early negotiations with their Irish counterparts so as to review the constitutional status of Northern Ireland, as the Cabinet felt that 'the reunification of the national territory can provide the only solution for the problem'. A four member Government sub-committee was also set up to deal with Northern Ireland policy. Its members were Joe Brennan, Padraig Faulkner, Charles Haughey and Neil Blaney. A fund for relief in the North was established under the control of Haughey, while an international propaganda campaign to promote the idea of Irish unity was given the go-ahead.

Lynch delivered his historic speech on television that same evening. He told those watching that, 'The Irish Government can no longer stand by and see innocent people injured'. In an interview with Joe Jackson in 1990 Blaney claimed that, 'that speech was composed word for word, every comma, every iota, as a collective Cabinet speech. It was not Jack Lynch's speech, made on behalf of his Government. It was a Cabinet speech, made by Jack Lynch'. This was the only statement on Northern Ireland policy which was discussed in any great detail at Cabinet during the time up to the ministerial dismissals in May of the following year.

Kevin Boland was still unhappy with the decisions proposed by the Government. Indeed, Boland had been disillusioned with the direction in which Fianna Fáil had been moving over the previous number of years, particularly in terms of both its policy on partition and also economic development. Boland's father was one of the founding fathers of the party and had served in Cabinet until 1957, at which time he stood aside and his son, Kevin, was appointed a Minister on his first day as a member of the Dáil. Kevin Boland would have preferred a Fianna Fáil with much more emphasis on its republicanism and less reliance on the free market as the means of achieving economic advancement. 'I didn't really realise it until 1969 when I looked around the Cabinet table and saw a no-good pathetic lot,' Boland says, and to the shock of his colleagues at Cabinet he tendered his resignation as he stormed from the Cabinet meeting. Blaney was one of those colleagues who went to Boland's home in an unsuccessful attempt to persuade him to change his mind. It took the intervention of President Eamon de Valera, however, to get Boland to withdraw his resignation. He did so then only on the understanding that he would no longer participate at Cabinet on issues regarding Northern Ireland. Occasionally, however, when Northern Ireland policy did arise at Cabinet meetings, Boland would pass notes to Blaney with his opinions written on them. 'I made a mental resolution that for the remainder of my time in Government I would speak no word about the Six Counties at Government meetings . . . I admit, however, that I often helped (or endeavoured to help) Blaney out with scribbled notes.'

For the remainder of 1969 and early 1970, the violence in Northern Ireland abated somewhat and there was hope that the proposed reforms in the North's system of Local Government would restore permanent order. Blaney had little faith in the various promises of reform and said that he believed that they would not be carried out. He was also critical of the decision to establish the Ulster Defence Regiment, which he perceived as putting 'the B Specials back in business'. He added that, 'The very name is a perpetuation of the entire sham that is the Six Counties while to me, as a free Ulsterman, it is a calculated insult'. A reliable Fine Gael source recalls 'being confused by Blaney's position at that time over the dominating role of the Unionists. In Donegal the plum positions went to Fianna Fáil people. And, without doubt, the plumest of the plum jobs went to Neil Blaney's people. To my mind, Blaney was simply practising the same discriminatory thing as the Unionists over the Border'.

Throughout this time, the confused Government position on Northern Ireland was evident. These divisions on Northern Ireland policy came sharply into the open in early December 1969. At a Donegal North East function in Letterkenny, to mark the 21st anniversary of his election to Dáil Éireann, Neil Blaney said that had the violent situation in Derry and Belfast the previous August continued, then the question of the use of force in defence of the nationalist community 'would have had to be urgently considered'. Two months previously the Taoiseach, Jack Lynch, in a speech in Tralee stated that, 'We are not seeking to overthrow by violence the Stormont Parliament or Government but rather to win the agreement of a sufficient number of people in the North to an acceptable form of reunification'. What Blaney said that night in Letterkenny was in fact not new. He had been delivering similar speeches at 'private' Fianna Fáil Party meetings over the preceding

THE FIANNA FÁIL PARTY 1927
Neal Blaney at de Valera's right shoulder.

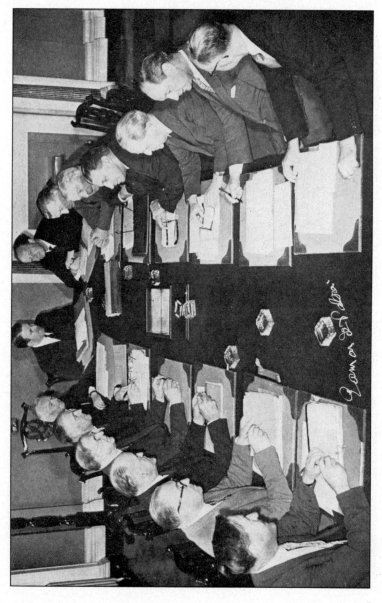

The last Cabinet meeting over which Eamon de Valera presided as Taoiseach, in 1959. Neil Blaney is seated at the head of the table next to Erskine Childers.

Seán F. Lemass presides over the first meeting of his new Cabinet in June 1959. Neil Blaney is standing directly behind him.

Neil Blaney, a profile photograph from the 1960s. (The Donegal Democrat)

Neil Blaney along with co-accused Charles Haughey arriving at Dublin District Court on 2 July 1970.
(The Irish Times)

Neil Blaney with Gerry Jones on his right at the Arms Trial. (The Irish Times)

Neil Blaney, former Minister for Agriculture and Fisheries, being carried from the District Court on 2 July 1970, after charges against him of importing arms were dropped.

'That was the year that was!'

Cartoon by J. Cogan that appeared in Hibernia, 8 January 1971.

months, the contents of which had seeped back to journalists and others by word of mouth. What was different about Letterkenny was that Blaney's speech was scripted and made publicly available. The divisions in Cabinet were now open for all to see.

In the address to his supporters Blaney said that, 'I believe, as do the vast majority, that the ideal way of ending partition is by peaceful means. But no one has the right to assert that force is irrevocably out. No political party or group at any time is entitled to predetermine the right of the Irish people to decide what course of action on this question may be justified in given circumstances. The Fianna Fáil Party has never taken a decision to rule out the use of force, if the circumstances in the Six Counties so demand . . . If a situation were to arise in the Six Counties in which the people who do not subscribe to the Unionist regime were under sustained and murderous assault, then, as the Taoiseach said on August 13th, we "cannot stand idly by".'

Kevin Boland was among a group of Ministers and TDs who made the trip to Letterkenny to celebrate Neil Blaney's 21st anniversary as a Dáil deputy. Boland says of Neil Blaney's address that night, 'His speech was well prepared and well circulated. I don't ever remember having seen him actually reading a speech before or since, but he had decided in advance what he wanted to say and he was making sure he said it and nothing else'.

Given the obvious conflict with Lynch's explicit ruling out of force, there were calls from the Opposition parties for Blaney's resignation. Conor Cruise O'Brien asserted that with Blaney's continued presence at Cabinet, the credibility of Jack Lynch's sentiments in his Tralee speech was totally destroyed. The Labour deputy added that he believed Blaney's Letterkenny speech to be 'the most irresponsible and demagogic statement made in recent times in this island with the sole exception of those by Mr Paisley'. It is fair to say that a Taoiseach in a stronger position than Jack Lynch would have sought Neil Blaney's immediate resignation. Lynch's position, however, was not a strong one and he responded to the speech by saying, 'While Mr Blaney's feelings on the partition issue are very deeply felt, and he occasionally finds it difficult not to give public expression to them, he knows and endorses Government policy on this issue, as he did in his speech in Letterkenny'. *The Irish Times*, in an editorial, said that, 'Mr Blaney is a fundamentalist,' although it went on to say that, 'Most people on this side of the Border, and many on the other side, even including some Unionists, will agree with him when he says that there cannot ever be a normal situation in the North while the Six Counties are a separate entity to the Twenty-six.' Nevertheless, John Hume saw fit to condemn Blaney's speech, describing it as 'totally irresponsible' and lacking in any solution to the problems of Northern Ireland. Hume added, 'It ill-becomes Mr Blaney to be divisive'.

What emerges from the Cabinet reaction to the events in the North was the divided nature of Lynch's Government. These divisions, however, went deeper than policy differences on Northern Ireland. What was also at play was the prolonged leadership battle in Fianna Fáil which had begun when Seán Lemass retired as Taoiseach in 1966. On RTE radio's 'This Week' programme, after his Letterkenny speech, Blaney denied that there was division within Cabinet on Northern Ireland, although, significantly, when asked if he would be interested in the position of Taoiseach he replied, 'If there was a situation which there was a Taoiseach being sought for the party and that the party wished to consider me, well then, in all possibility, I would have to consider very seriously the implications of that and leave it to the party's best judgement, as has been done in the past in a fair selection'.

Regardless of Blaney's comments that there was total loyalty to the Taoiseach at that time, it is obvious that Jack Lynch was still perceived by the major players in Fianna Fáil as a short-term leader. He still did not have enough supporters at Cabinet and he was unable to put his own stamp on Government policy. His tussles with Neil Blaney over agricultural matters and his abortive attempts to move the Agriculture Minister to a new Planning Department after the 1969 general election, are just two examples of the relatively weak position in which Lynch found himself. He may have been electorally successful in the 1969 general election, but the masterminds behind that success were Haughey and Blaney. It is fascinating to observe, however, that within little over a year of the outbreak of violence in Northern Ireland, Jack Lynch most certainly became his own man, probably for the first time since his election as Taoiseach in 1966. Kevin Boland has contended that Jack Lynch set up Blaney and Haughey to get them out of Cabinet. While this opinion lacks any substantial evidence, it is probably true to say that Jack Lynch made the best use of the events of the Arms Crisis for his own political motives. By the time of the 1971 Fianna Fáil Ard-Fheis Jack Lynch was totally in control. Boland was gone, Haughey was toeing the line and Blaney was a marginalised figure, stripped of power, on the verge of extinction as a member of Fianna Fáil.

The republican caucus in Cabinet believed, however, that if soldiers from the Republic went into the North, they would create an international incident, which would bring UN intervention and provoke serious moves on the issue of partition. While this view may not have been officially adopted, it is obvious that some of the decisions taken by the Cabinet in early August 1969 did not remove entirely the idea of military intervention. The Government policy on Northern Ireland over this period is one of ambivalence, and the failure of the Cabinet at this time to discuss Northern Ireland in any length or detail is most certainly unusual. Any serious analysis of the events which make up the Arms Crisis is fraught with difficulty, not least because the main participants openly contradict each other in their interpretation of events. What is certain, however, is that Jack Lynch abdicated responsibility for policy on Northern Ireland after August 1969. It is, as Blaney says, almost as if Lynch did not want to know. Lynch had given central roles to men whose opinions on Northern policy were totally at odds with his own and because of this much blame for the activities which occurred must be shouldered by him. Vincent Browne, in his 1980 *Magill* series on the Arms Crisis, argues that responsibility for what happened 'lies with

Jack Lynch, not because of any deviousness or duplicity on his part, as some of his enemies would like to allege, rather because of an indecisiveness and weakness which was responsible for a great deal of the chaos that ensued'.

Despite the contentions of Neil Blaney that an armed intervention by Irish troops into Derry or Newry was desirable, the fact remains that the army was ill-equipped for any serious intervention in Northern Ireland. In addition, any interventionist policy along the Border, even if only carried out to create an incident which would precipitate UN involvement, would have left the Catholics in West Belfast exposed and totally vulnerable to loyalist attack. Despite this reality, Blaney argued at Cabinet for such action and has lamented ever since the decision not to intervene. 'The decision to send the army to the Border was taken deliberately. Most of us believed the army would cross over, particularly into Derry . . . that would have precipitated UN intervention immediately.'

The Cabinet debate at the time is recalled by Brian Lenihan. 'Blaney felt highly emotionally involved, and committed, living near the Border. He had never made a secret of his feelings. He was impatient and anxious to help in as positive a way as possible, on a face-to-face basis. He felt that genuinely. There was no question of using the situation for a leadership feud. That didn't arise. Blaney held a different concept and view of the problem from Lynch's. Blaney was more direct, more forthright, more aggressive, more go at it – whereas Lynch was more laid back . . . he took on the role, as he saw it, as Taoiseach of the country *vis-a-vis* his responsibilities to the country as a whole. Blaney saw the situation in terms of Northern Ireland, defending the nationalists in Northern Ireland and showing them some active evidence of support.'

The Cabinet gave Charles Haughey and Jim Gibbons, the Minister for Defence, responsibility for assessing the military needs of the army, while men from Derry were to receive training in the use of weapons from the FCA at Fort Dunree, in County Donegal.

Following media interest in what was going on in Dunree, the operation was cancelled and the existence of the training camp was only formally revealed during the Arms Trial. Lynch was to say that, 'They were Irish citizens and they were entitled to join the defence forces'. The question that has to be asked, however, is why train these men from the North in the use of such weapons if they were not going to be provided with such weapons?

Two other episodes occurred: the Ballymurphy arms movement and Gibbons' February directive to the army, which clearly illustrate, as Dunree does, the lack of a clearly thought out policy in relation to Northern Ireland on the part of either Lynch or the Government he led. In such an environment it is no wonder the Arms Plot could be seen by some to be within Government policy. When rioting occurred in Ballymurphy on 2 April 1970 some five hundred rifles were moved from the Curragh to Dundalk. Jim Gibbons was, according to *Magill* magazine, 'entirely at a loss to explain at the Arms Trial why there should have been the movement of these guns to Dundalk unless there were at least the vague possibility that they might be shipped across the Border into the hands of civilians'. Neil Blaney recalls the Ballymurphy incident. 'Two army units set out on their way to Belfast but were stopped in Dundalk. In the meantime the situation that had brought about their departure from Dublin abated and the trucks didn't go in. Of course nobody will ever agree that they were there. And nobody ever can tell you where they went after they left Dundalk. Did they turn back? Did they bury them? Destroy them?'

Blaney also says that one of the two trucks was loaded totally with arms and the other with gas masks, among other equipment. In February 1970 a controversial, and disputed, Government directive on Northern Ireland was issued by Jim Gibbons to the army. This directive advised the army 'that plans be immediately put in train for operating in Northern Ireland, in the event of the situation (in the opinion of the Government) warrants interference'.

It was this flurry of activity by the Dublin Government, along with Lynch's promise not to 'stand (idly) by', which combined to give the impression in the North that the Irish Government was on the verge of directly intervening in the Six Counties. When the violence erupted in the North, delegations, including MPs at the Stormont Parliament, came to Dublin requesting arms to defend the nationalist community. Several TACA businessmen are reported to have offered financial resources to groups in the North for the purchase of arms. Guns from all sorts of reasonable and respectable people in the Republic were being offered to nationalists in the North. There is a story told of one Fianna Fáil TD from Cork who brought guns in the boot of his car into the car-park in Leinster House, from where they were moved into the boot of a car of a Fianna Fáil senator from a Northern county, and then smuggled into the Six Counties. It is against this type of background that the Arms Crisis must be set. There was enormous sympathy for the plight of the nationalist community in the North and people in the South were responding to the situation in the most effective way, as they saw it.

The atmosphere in the country, both North and South, was emotional and one of confusion. The IRA, which had moved away from military activity, was itself divided in its approach to the emergence of violence. It was attracting a large influx of new members. In December 1969, a split took place in the IRA producing the Official and Provisional wings of the IRA. Blaney has blamed Lynch for the creation of the Provisionals. People who were later identified as leaders of the IRA, were among the delegations that came to Dublin, Blaney says, ultimately seeking arms. 'And after one of the last meetings, I remember they came back to my office after meeting with Lynch and they were highly confident that they were getting what they wanted. But I said to them, "Don't go overboard on what you believe you have been promised".' Blaney feels that the expectations of these people were heightened and when they were not realised they lost faith in the *bona fide* concern of the Dublin Government to protect them and so they took up arms to do so themselves. Ironically, Neil Blaney, himself, has been linked with the establishment of the Provisionals, although as one political journalist remarked, 'Blaney had absolutely no part in setting up the Provos and any talk on his behalf that he had are simply pretensions on his part'.

At the Fianna Fáil Ard-Fheis in January 1970 Jack Lynch told his party's delegates that, 'We may feel with our hearts, but we must think with our heads, and when the heart rules the head, the voice of wisdom goes unheard'. Lynch again ruled out force, but the views of several of his most Senior Ministers were, at that time, contrary to those of the Taoiseach who, it would seem, was oblivious to the events that were occurring around him.

The plan to import arms, which was the centre of the Arms Trial, began at a meeting held in Baileboro, County Cavan, on 4 October 1969. The Gardai Special Branch monitored a meeting in Baileboro between Captain James Kelly, an army intelligence officer, and known subversives from Northern Ireland. This information was passed on to Peter Berry, the Secretary of the Department of Justice, who was at that time receiving medical treatment in the Mount Carmel nursing home in Dublin. Berry was unable to contact either his own Minister, Micheál O'Moráin, or the Taoiseach, although he did succeed in contacting Charles Haughey with whom he had worked before, when Haughey was Justice Minister. Haughey, who was then the Minister for Finance, met Berry at Mount Carmel and Berry relayed his information to him. When Berry eventually got to speak to Jack Lynch it was in connection with further information concerning the Baileboro meeting. This information was that Captain Kelly had allegedly promised money and assistance in importing arms to known members of the IRA. A figure of £50,000 was allegedly promised by Captain Kelly for the purchase of arms.

Jack Lynch was later to deny that he was ever given details of the Baileboro meeting by Berry. However, several days later the Minister for Defence, Jim Gibbons, asked Colonel Hefferon, the Director of

Military Intelligence, what Captain Kelly was doing in Baileboro. Although Gibbons said later that he was never told of the meeting, it would appear that Lynch had conveyed details of his meeting with Berry to Jim Gibbons. The Minister for Justice, Micheál O'Moráin, maintained that he told Jack Lynch in December 1969 of information he received from the Special Branch, implicating Haughey and Blaney in a plot to import arms. Lynch denied that O'Moráin ever conveyed such information. Indeed, to this day, Jack Lynch maintains that he only first heard of the Arms Plot on 20 April 1970 when Peter Berry brought the attempted plot to his attention.

In April 1970, Berry received information that an attempt was about to be made to import several tons of arms. Blaney and Haughey were said to be involved. Captain James Kelly saw himself as fulfilling an intermediary role between Blaney and Haughey and those in the North seeking arms. He travelled to a number of countries where he met with arms dealers in efforts to acquire arms. Captain Kelly was accompanied on several of these trips by Albert Luykx, a Belgian businessman and associate of Neil Blaney, who acted as an interpreter. The army intelligence officer was also accompanied, on other occasions, by John Kelly from Belfast, no relation, who was his principal contact in Northern Ireland and the main organiser of the citizens defence committees throughout the Six Counties. An earlier attempt to import arms from the United States had been scuttled, according to Vincent Browne in *Magill*, as Neil Blaney had arranged a deal on the continent. Browne states that, 'Blaney by now had assumed a central role in the entire affair and he was to direct operations in relation to the purchase of arms henceforth'.

Captain Kelly, with the assistance of Luykx, struck a deal with a German arms dealer to supply arms with £35,000 from the relief fund administered by Haughey. The Dáil had sanctioned a sum of £100,000 for relief in Northern Ireland. Some of this money was used to finance, contrary to the wishes of the Taoiseach, a publication, *The Voice of the North*, which was edited by Seamus Brady, a friend of Neil Blaney. It was Brady who, the previous September, had introduced Captain Kelly to Neil Blaney and it was Blaney, in turn, who had introduced Kelly to Charles Haughey.

According to Gerry Jones, the Bandon born businessman, who became nationally known during the Arms Trial when he was described as Blaney's 'shadow', Blaney's involvement stemmed from the fact that 'he was very concerned. His principal concern from the outset was that lives would be saved and that people could get shelter . . . and that was the purpose of his visit, and my visit, to the North with the £100,000. What the people wanted was money to refurnish and set up their homes again. Blaney saw that quite clearly and then we were accused of using it, the £100,000, to buy arms. Some of it may have been used to buy arms, I don't know . . .' Blaney himself told *The Sunday Business Post* that 'the £100,000 was accounted for, I have no doubt. My attitude towards the £100,000 was that you feed somebody who's hungry lest they die of starvation, you clothe them with blankets lest they die of the cold. Why not buy a gun for them to protect themselves from the killer?' John Kelly in an unsworn statement in court in October 1970 said, however, 'We did not ask for blankets or feeding bottles, we asked for guns. And no one, from the Taoiseach Lynch down, refused us that request or told us this was contrary to Government policy'. Three months after the Arms Trial ended, the Dáil Public Accounts Committee conducted an extensive inquiry into the spending of the £100,000 sanctioned for the Northern Ireland Relief Fund. It discovered that apart from £32,000 used to purchase German arms, a further £34,000 had been spent for 'undetermined purposes' in Belfast. It has been suggested that much of this money was used to establish the Provisional IRA, a suggestion that Neil Blaney emphatically denies.

Over the months leading up to April 1970, several abortive attempts had been made to import arms into the country. In the second last week of April 1970, the last and most determined efforts were made to import arms. The plan was for the arms to be shipped from Germany to Dublin before they were taken to the Six Counties. The Arms Plot unravelled because of difficulties with transport and import documentation. Dublin Airport was surrounded by the Special Branch and when those involved received news of this, they once again called off the importation. Peter Berry approached Lynch who at first appeared reluctant to believe the evidence, but indicated his intention to confront both Haughey and Blaney. The following day, April 22, was Budget Day and with Haughey injured in a horse riding accident, the Taoiseach had to deliver the Budget speech on Haughey's behalf. Therefore, Lynch put off an immediate confrontation with both Ministers. In fact, Jack Lynch did not see Haughey until almost a week later, even though it is known that Neil Blaney, among others, saw Haughey in hospital prior to the Taoiseach's visit.

On the afternoon of 23 April, a meeting took place in Neil Blaney's office in Leinster House. Captain James Kelly and Jim Gibbons were present. The meeting was held to discuss the implications for those involved in the arms importation from Special Branch investigations and Revenue Commissioners inquiries. Blaney is said to have remarked that it really did not matter who investigated the attempted importation as no guns had been brought into the country and therefore there could be no prosecutions.

On Wednesday 29 April, Jack Lynch summoned Neil Blaney to his office and confronted him with the information he had, regarding the Minister for Agriculture's involvement in the attempted arms' importation. Blaney denied any involvement and refused Lynch's request for his resignation. 'Nothing doing. Forget about it, I'm not resigning. I've done nothing. Why should I resign?' is what Blaney says he told Lynch. Lynch let the matter lie with Blaney and then he went to see Haughey who was still recovering in hospital. The actual content of this meeting is still unknown, as Haughey never revealed what transpired. It is not clear if Lynch asked for Haughey's resignation. Lynch is reported, in *Magill* magazine, as saying that Haughey was too unwell to speak, although he told the Dáil on 10 May 1970 that Haughey asked for some time to consider his position. Neil Blaney has said that he himself spoke with Haughey after his own meeting with the Taoiseach, to inform him of Lynch's request and he says of Haughey's 'inability to talk' – 'The bastard would have choked him, never mind anything else'.

The next day, 30 April, Jack Lynch told Peter Berry that he had met with both Haughey and Blaney and that the matter was closed. At a Cabinet meeting the following day, Lynch is reported to have told his Ministers that allegations had been made against two members of the Government, both of whom had denied any involvement, and that the issue was closed. It would appear that Lynch was prepared to end the issue at that stage. After the Cabinet meeting Boland went to inform Haughey of the news but, despite the Taoiseach's apparent intention to drop the resignation request, Neil Blaney, who attended the Cabinet meeting, was not so convinced that the last had been heard on the subject. A few days later in the Dáil, during the debate on the Budget, Blaney told Michael O'Leary of the Labour Party that, 'We are going to be here (next year), bar some strange, extraordinary happening, and there could be one'. O'Leary asked of the Minister for Agriculture, 'An earthquake?' to which Blaney replied, 'No, but it could be next door to it'.

Neil Blaney was to be proved right. On the evening of 5 May 1970 he was chairing a meeting of the Fianna Fáil National Organising Committee in the party's rooms in Leinster House. At a quarter to ten, he received a note asking him to meet the Taoiseach immediately. Kevin Boland, who was sitting next to Blaney, says in his book, *We won't stand (idly) by*, that Blaney passed the note on to him and said, 'What did I tell you? This is it. Will you take over the chair?'.

Boland concluded the meeting without delay and went straight to the Parliamentary Secretaries' dining room where he sat with Paudge Brennan, awaiting the return of the Minister for Agriculture. Brennan, a deputy representing Wicklow since 1954, was Parliamentary Secretary at the Department of Local Government where Boland was the Senior Minister. When Blaney arrived he told them that Lynch had requested his resignation, to which he had replied that he would give his decision the following morning. Blaney said that Lynch had replied that he could not wait until then and that if the resignation was not forthcoming immediately, he would request that the President terminate Blaney's ministerial appointment. Kevin Boland immediately forwarded his own resignation to Lynch whose Cabinet was, in the space of a number of days, to lose four of its members. Micheál O'Moráin, who had been ill for some time, was obviously unable to cope with the ministerial duties and while he was in hospital on 4 May Lynch sought his resignation, to which the Mayo man is reported to have replied, 'You can have it here and now, go bugger off for yourself'.

It would seem that Jack Lynch had been rattled into action earlier that same evening, at eight o'clock, after a meeting with Liam Cosgrave, the Fine Gael leader. Cosgrave had received information that Haughey and Blaney had allegedly been involved in an attempt to import arms. He had, in fact, received this information on the previous Thursday, 30 April, and after two anonymous attempts at getting the Independent Group newspapers to publish the story were unsuccessful, he went to Lynch. Neil Blaney claimed subsequently that the leak to Cosgrave came from the British Secret Service through some of their Irish counterparts. Although there is no public evidence to prove this allegation, Blaney refers to a meeting which Jack Lynch had with the British Ambassador prior to the arrests, along with other information he himself later received. Whatever decision the Taoiseach had taken the previous week about allowing the whole affair to subside was, with Cosgrave's knowledge of the events, rendered null and void. Within six hours of the Fine Gael leader's intervention, Blaney and Haughey had been dismissed and the country was faced with a crisis of monumental proportions.

After requesting Blaney's resignation Jack Lynch proceeded to telephone Haughey, who was at his home in Kinsealy. Neither Lynch nor Haughey have ever discussed the contents of this conversation. Following this conversation with Haughey, Jack Lynch went home to his wife Maureen. At about 12.15 a.m. the first indication of potential drama came when Eoin Neeson, who was head of the Government Information Services, telephoned newspaper offices and asked how long they could hold their papers for a story. Neeson did not say what the story was, but at 2.50 a.m. the official statement was released. It had been dictated to Neeson over the phone by Lynch some time earlier.

The statement read: 'I have requested the resignations as members of the Government of Mr Neil T. Blaney, Minister for Agriculture and Fisheries, and Mr Charles J. Haughey, Minister for Finance, because I am satisfied that they do not subscribe fully to Government policy in relation to the present situation in the Six Counties, as stated by me at the Fianna Fáil Ard-Fheis in January last'.

— 5 —
Sacked

Neil Blaney's ministerial career which began with his appointment to Cabinet by Eamon de Valera in 1957 was ended on the morning of 6 May 1970. The beginning of the end of his career in Fianna Fáil was also set in motion with this dismissal from Cabinet.

All the daily newspapers led with the startling news that Jack Lynch's Government had lost three Senior Ministers. Amid all the revelations, the Dáil was adjourned until 10 p.m. that evening so as to facilitate a meeting of the Fianna Fáil Parliamentary Party which was scheduled for 6.00 p.m. During the day rumour and counter rumour spread through Leinster House, with talk rampant of a general election. Neil Blaney and his supporters usually occupied a table beside the coat-stand in the member's restaurant that had acquired the nickname of 'the hat-rack parliament'. It was also known as the 'Letterkenny Parliament' because it was there that Blaney sat with his two Donegal senators, Bernard McGlinchey and Paddy McGowan. To be seen near this table on 6 May was to bring suspicion that one was involved with Blaney.

At the Parliamentary Party meeting, Lynch presented the assembled members with the choice of either supporting him in the decision he had taken or else facing the prospect of a general election in which many could expect to lose their seats. Blaney recalls jumping to his feet at the meeting to say that Lynch had indeed the right to hire and fire Ministers and that that was not at issue.

'A bloody crisis meeting so that he could come in with this stupid thing that was provided for in the goddamn Constitution. He has the right, as Taoiseach, to hire and fire. There was no need for a crisis meeting. So I was on my feet immediately, to say, "Look, there's nobody questioning it, we're being fired. You hire, you fire and that's it.".'

Blaney has also said with some humour that one reason why the meeting finished so rapidly was that, 'Celtic were playing the feckin' Cup Final and I wanted to see it'. Blaney is, in fact, an avid soccer supporter and he served for several years as President of the Football Association of Ireland.

'The sacking of Mr Haughey and Mr Blaney, and Mr Boland's resignation seem this morning almost certainly to lead to a general election,' so wrote Dick Walsh in *The Irish Times* of 6 May 1970. He had not allowed for Fianna Fáil's ability to unite in the tightest of corners. Nevertheless, unity in the face of such turmoil caused surprise. Arthur Noonan, who was RTE's political reporter, observed that, 'The news that the Fianna Fáil Party has fixed everything up after no more than fifty minutes, that the ranks had been closed and that the smiles were back on all faces came as quite an anti-climax to the long hours of tension and build-up during which deputies sought any bits and pieces of information as eagerly as members of the public'. The thought of losing their seats in an election was enough to shake Fianna Fáil deputies into support for Lynch and the direction he was taking. Nevertheless, despite all the papering over the cracks, great bitterness and resentment was simmering only just marginally below the surface as Des O'Malley admits, 'Things got very, very bitter and the atmosphere was very unpleasant and tense. It did split Fianna Fáil, maybe not there and then in terms of voting numbers in the Dáil, but it did split Fianna Fáil and in a sense the party has never recovered'.

When the Dáil assembled Lynch outlined why he had dismissed Blaney and Haughey. He said that he had information which purported to connect the two former Ministers with being involved in an attempted illegal importation of arms from Europe. The highly charged debate continued until three o'clock that morning and when a vote was called there were scuffles in the voting lobby during the division. The following day, 7 May, at a dinner given by the Fianna Fáil organisation in Laois, Jack Lynch referred to the dismissed Ministers as 'able, brilliant and dedicated men'. When the

Dáil reconvened on 8 May the debate on the appointment of the Ministers to fill the vacancies caused by the exit from Cabinet of Boland, Haughey and Blaney lasted for a marathon thirty-six hours. Neil Blaney denied any involvement or knowledge of any plot to import arms. His emotional address to the Dáil began with frankness and bluntness. 'I want straightaway to deal with the allegations of gun-running that have been so freely made in so many places these last few days and to say here before this House that I have run no guns, I have procured no guns, I have paid for no guns, I have provided no money to buy guns and anybody who says otherwise is not telling the truth.'

Nevertheless, despite his dismissal, Blaney confirmed his support for Lynch and the Government. 'I could not but be Fianna Fáil and republican unless I was to renege the heritage of my parents before me.' When he sat down the applause from the Fianna Fáil benches was the loudest received by any speaker throughout the debate. Blaney used his speech to indirectly attack Lynch by lambasting the Opposition parties. In the debate which followed, Opposition deputies rounded on Blaney as he, and the speech which he had delivered, came in for ridicule. Dr Noel Browne said, 'I can only describe Deputy Blaney's speech today as an evil speech. It was a terrible speech. It was an appallingly irresponsible speech'. Garret FitzGerald spoke of 'a sinister, ruthless, ambitious man' who he believed was 'a man of remarkable ability – ability which is not always well used'.

In *The Irish Times* the following day John Healy wrote, 'Mr Blaney's speech was extremely cleverly worded: he has shown himself capable, even in a crisis situation, of tooling words and phrases which are capable of a number of interpretations: it is possible for instance, to construe the attack on Fine Gael and its peace policy on the North as an indirect attack on Mr Lynch'. Healy went on to say that, 'It was an emotional speech designed to be heard and read by the grassroots: it would have been a great speech at the Ard Fheis or in his father's day thirty or forty years ago'.

Blaney's explicit and emphatic denial of any involvement in the Arms Affair led Labour's Justin Keating to say of him, 'Either he is a sincere and honest man who has been framed or else he is a polished and total liar'. Charlie Haughey later denied that he took any part in the arms importation or that he knew anything about it. Captain James Kelly, John Kelly and Albert Luykx all denied that the attempted importation was illegal. Captain Kelly said that the Ministers had full knowledge of what was occurring. He claimed that Jim Gibbons, Minister for Defence, was fully aware and was kept informed of all activities that he had been involved in. Captain Kelly said at the time that, 'Mr Gibbons had indicated on several occasions that I was doing an excellent job for the country as an intelligence officer'. Jim Gibbons, however, denied any involvement in the controversial events, a fact which was later to assume great importance.

Neil Blaney says that if he had to re-live these events again, he would act totally differently and bring down both Jack Lynch and his Government. He admitted in one interview that, 'The irony is that the very people who sustained the Government were the people that were blackened by the late Erskine Childers, his master's voice, speaking in the Dáil. Blackened, to frighten people into an acceptance that these were bad boys and that they had been stepping out of line and that there was going to be a *coup d'état*. We were the very people that defused that by going into the Fianna Fáil meeting which Lynch had concocted to assert his right, as Taoiseach, to hire and fire.' Gerry Jones believes that the loss of office was not a great disappointment to Blaney. 'I don't think that affected him half as much as the failure of the Taoiseach to recognise the seriousness of the situation' in Northern Ireland.

Some 3,000 people gathered in the Market Square in Letterkenny to welcome Neil Blaney home to Donegal on 15 May. It was Blaney's first appearance in the constituency since his dismissal. The route from Dublin had taken the former Minister through Northern Ireland despite a threat, allegedly by the UVF, that if he entered the Six Counties he would not leave it alive. Blaney was met at Monaghan by a motorcade of almost one hundred cars. On the journey through Northern Ireland the motorcade was escorted by British Army armoured cars. When they reached the Donegal border, Blaney was carried shoulder high from the British Customs post at Strabane across the bridge into Lifford where he was greeted by cheering supporters. Blaney spoke of being 'back among my own people' while he added that he believed that, 'The Fianna Fáil organisation is stronger to-day than it was this night week'.

On 28 May, Neil Blaney was arrested on arms conspiracy charges and released on bail. He was charged, along with four others, with conspiring to import arms and ammunition into the State between 1 March and 24 April 1970. His four co-defendants were Charles Haughey, Captain James Kelly, Albert Luykx and John Kelly. This action was in contravention of the *Firearms Acts* and was therefore considered an offence contrary to common law. Liam Hamilton, who was later to chair the Beef Tribunal, led Blaney's legal team and after reading the book of evidence presented for the case Hamilton declared it a 'book of no evidence'. In Blaney's case the description was an apt one, for when the case came before the Dublin District Court on 2 July 1970, he was freed. District Justice Donal Kearney said that the points raised by Liam Hamilton for Blaney had also occurred to him and that after reading the book of evidence he accepted that there was not sufficient evidence to justify him returning Blaney on a conspiracy charge. 'I am returning the other four men for trial and I am refusing informations against Mr. Blaney,' he added.

Neil Blaney was overcome with emotion as he left the court house to meet supporters and friends after the case against him was dismissed in July 1970. He was hoisted up on their shoulders and carried in celebration from the District Court, with over thirty Irish and foreign journalists following in eager pursuit. An impromptu press conference was held near-by in the middle of Chancery Street. Blaney said, 'I am delighted and feel very much vindicated'. Outside the court house Blaney's wife, Eva, spoke of her delight at the outcome — 'It is not really a surprise, I am very happy'. When pressed by one journalist whether he would be prepared to serve again under Jack Lynch as Taoiseach, Blaney replied curtly – 'I'll have to think about that'. There was a massive celebration that night and one source recalls that Liam Hamilton, who represented Blaney, was 'proud as punch' with the outcome.

Blaney's position in the Arms Crisis came in for severe criticism in the *Magill* Arms Crisis issues, published in July 1980. Vincent Browne, the author of these articles, asserted that 'It was he (Blaney) who was the main instigator of the entire operation. It was he, effectively, to whom Captain Kelly reported and of course it was he who got Albert Luykx involved. Yet, when the whole thing blew up, Blaney simply denied his involvement, leaving Kelly and Luykx to their own devices'. Browne admits that Neil Blaney's denial to the Dáil that he had guns, procured guns, paid for guns or provided money for the purchase of guns is essentially true, 'but that the impression of a blanket denial which he obviously intended to convey wasn't of great assistance to Kelly or Luykx'. If Blaney had acknowledged his own involvement in the attempted importation and had defended this position Vincent Browne feels that 'the public perception of what had happened would have been much clearer and perhaps Kelly and Luykx would not have been prosecuted at all'.

The defence lawyers in the Arms Trial, acting on behalf of the accused, met prior to the trial and they discussed whether to call Neil Blaney as a witness for Haughey and the others who had been returned for trial. In the end they decided not to call Blaney. The fact that Blaney did not take the witness stand during the Arms Trial is certainly unusual – given his alleged central involvement in the entire affair. While Blaney's own case had been thrown out by the District Court, the reason for his Cabinet dismissal still stood as his involvement in an attempted arms importation. Blaney would probably have been in a position to corroborate the contention of

Luykz and Kelly that the importation had official sanction and, therefore, that their actions were in fact legal. On this issue Blaney says: 'It was so obvious that I should have been in the witness box. I attended every moment of every session of both the abortive trial and the trial and I am still wondering why I wasn't called'. Vincent Browne believes that one of the main reasons why Blaney was not called by the defence to give evidence was because, 'it was felt it was too difficult to predict what exactly he would say under cross-examination'. Neil Blaney himself feels that the initial difference in the approach of the defence lawyers for the accused, after the serving of the book of evidence, may explain why he was not called. Blaney feels that, like himself, the others should have contested the charge and that they would then probably not have been returned for trial.

Blaney's actions during the months after his case was dismissed were both cautious and calculated. Although he followed the party line in Dáil divisions, his public speeches were laced with coded messages reflective of his differences with Jack Lynch's policy on Northern Ireland. According to Kevin Boland, Jack Lynch and his supporters used these summer months to consolidate their hold over the Fianna Fáil organisation, travelling throughout the country to identify loyalists and eliminate dissidents. Blaney obviously still remained a threat to Lynch, but his failure to take effective action in light of his Cabinet dismissal placed him increasingly on the periphery of the party.

Kevin Boland failed in his attempts in the immediate aftermath of the events of May 1970 to get Blaney and Haughey to join with him in calling a special Ard-Fheis to fight Jack Lynch and return the republican ethos to Fianna Fáil. Des O'Malley, who was appointed Minister for Justice in May 1970, recalls that there were some apprehensions about the intentions of the three former Ministers. A united challenge from Boland, Blaney and Haughey could have had serious consequences for Jack Lynch's leadership. 'I don't think that there was a fear that Blaney personally would do it, but it was thought that he might organise some others to do it and I suppose the one thought most likely to do it was Haughey,' O'Malley admits.

The mutual distrust which existed between Haughey and Blaney, however, killed off all attempts to formulate a joint approach in response to the dismissals. According to Kevin Boland, 'Blaney and Haughey were watching each other. They didn't trust each other'. Boland adds that, 'There was no getting them together. Each wanted to be sure they would be Taoiseach. I'd say Blaney's motivation there would be that he wanted to be sure that the character of the organisation would be republican. He wasn't by no means certain of Haughey, despite their circumstances. I really don't believe that Blaney had any personal ambition to be Taoiseach. His ambition was that the organisation remained a republican organisation. He would have been just as pleased, I think, to have been Tánaiste so long as the Tánaiste had a new role as a disciplining authority that was badly needed. Blaney didn't see anyone he could trust. The only one he would trust would be me and I would never have touched the job, never, with a forty foot pole, no way'.

Charles Haughey's involvement in the Arms Affair came as a total shock to most people. Des O'Malley recalls being 'totally shocked' when he learned that Haughey had been linked with arms importation allegations. While Blaney later says that his friendship with Haughey was one-sided and that he was a good friend of Haughey while Haughey used him, it is obvious that Blaney was deeply suspicious of Haughey's motivations in 1969-70. Gerry Jones believes that Blaney was probably right. 'I think with hindsight that Haughey maybe had a secondary purpose and he saw in it, in my opinion, the possibility of acquiring power – the leadership.'

Initially, among their colleagues in Fianna Fáil, the ex-Ministers received sympathetic support, although in the end it proved to be almost totally superficial. Neil Blaney may have been awaiting a rush of outrage when a 'not guilty' verdict was announced at the Arms Trial which might have forced Jack Lynch to resign. In such a situation Fianna Fáil could have returned to the policy line on

Northern Ireland in which Blaney believed. Whatever hope there was of an end to Lynch's leadership all but disappeared after Haughey issued an abortive challenge to Lynch to resign, following his acquittal at the Arms Trial on 23 October 1970. Rather than generating sympathy for the former Ministers and a rally of support to their cause, Haughey's challenge was met with strong resistance. Jack Lynch returned from a visit to the United States three days after Haughey issued his challenge. He was met at Dublin Airport by a substantial contingent of the Fianna Fáil Parliamentary Party in a very public endorsement of his leadership.

What the aftermath of the Arms Trial did, however, was confirm in Neil Blaney's mind the singular motivation behind Haughey's involvement in the arms importation affair. Despite all the attempts by Kevin Boland to get Haughey and Blaney together to co-ordinate their actions, Haughey went his own way immediately after the acquittal verdict was announced. To the amazement of Neil Blaney and Kevin Boland, both of whom had attended every minute of the trial, Haughey had organised a press conference in the Ormond Hotel, beside the Four Courts. Neither of his two former colleagues had been informed or invited to take part. Gerry Jones who was also with Blaney recalls that Haughey 'had his own television show to go on the air and with no consultation'.

Whatever internal dissent there was, the large turn-out of support at Dublin Airport in October 1970 confirmed the consolidated position of Jack Lynch as leader of Fianna Fáil and the isolated role which the men dismissed some months earlier now played within the party. Blaney may have felt, after his own case was thrown out, that he was biding his time until Fianna Fáil publicly endorsed his policy positions. By October 1970 it was obvious that such a situation was unlikely to occur. The majority of Fianna Fáil TDs felt that their seats were safer under the leadership of Jack Lynch, who had succeeded in holding the party together throughout the crisis of the preceding months, than they would have been with any alignment with either Blaney or Haughey. For the average Fianna Fáil TD the question of the safety of his/her Dáil seat took precedence over any disputes concerning policy, even policy differences relating to partition and Northern Ireland.

The report of the Honorary Secretaries at the first post-Arms Trial Ard-Fheis in February 1971 merely referred to the events of the previous twelve months as 'internal difficulties which arose last year in the Organisation'. Paddy Hillery delivered a powerful speech which strongly backed Jack Lynch as leader of Fianna Fáil and his stance on Northern Ireland. There were many speeches from both factions within the party but, overall, it was evident that Lynch's personal dominance of Fianna Fáil had increased dramatically over the preceding twelve months. Haughey did not speak at the 1971 Ard-Fheis and he made only a brief appearance over the weekend. Kevin Boland attempted to speak as an ordinary delegate amid cheers and jeers as Blaney watched on from the platform. Blaney's contributions were confined to his duties as Honorary Treasurer of the party and contained no criticism of Jack Lynch. George Colley challenged Blaney for his position as Honorary Treasurer and successfully defeated the former Minister who had held this important party position since the mid-1950s and had, over this time, presided over substantial annual increases in the National Collection. Blaney attributes his loss to Gerry Collins who was involved in the change in voting procedures at the 1971 Ard-Fheis which, he feels, were introduced to ensure that he was defeated. From May 1970 onwards, it was clear that Jack Lynch was seeking to marginalise the position of Neil Blaney within Fianna Fáil. His removal as an officer of the party was another step in achieving that aim.

Blaney was also being put under pressure in other ways. His close friend and confidant, Gerry Jones, who had been appointed to the Board of Directors of Irish Shipping by Jack Lynch in 1965, was not reappointed when his term of office came to an end in June 1971. Jones, with a distinctive patch over his right eye, described his non-reappointment as a 'political move . . . because of my association with Mr Blaney'. On a more directly political level, Blaney was also discovering that letters he was writing to Government Departments on behalf of constituents were being replied to with a letter from his constituency colleague, Liam Cunningham, to the constituent. This was particularly so in relation to correspondence with the Department of Local Government, the Department to which Cunningham happened to be appointed as Parliamentary Secretary by Lynch in the wake of the May 1970 dismissals. The appointment was a strategic one by the Taoiseach to try to diminish Blaney's influence over the local party organisation, as well as attempting to quell potential disquiet over the sacking of Blaney.

Any attempt by Jack Lynch to reduce Neil Blaney's pivotal position in Donegal North East was, however, likely to prove difficult. A study of the Blaney political machine in the mid-1960s had illustrated the dominant position that Neil Blaney had assumed in the constituency. At the time of the study by Paul Sacks, there were sixty-seven registered Fianna Fáil cumainn in Donegal North East with an electorate of 37,371. Some twenty-five (37 per cent) of these cumainn were, however, concentrated on the Blaney base of Milford which had an electorate of 8,691 (23 per cent). With this, the largest single block of cumainn in the constituency, Blaney was in a position to effectively control the nomination of candidates for local and general elections. Prior to 1967, John Harkin, a Creeslough based county councillor, moved to live in Milford, thereby threatening the political terrain of the Blaneys as those disgruntled with the dominant position of Neil Blaney began to support Harkin. Blaney, however, flexed his muscles at the selection convention to choose the Fianna Fáil candidates for the 1967 local elections in the constituency. Fianna Fáil had previously run three candidates for the four seats in the Milford area, but in 1967 Blaney used his majority at the convention to decide that Fianna Fáil would put four candidates on the ticket. The strategy was to surround Harkin on all sides so that his vote would be reduced. Harkin, however, polled well, coming in second only to Harry Blaney. He was forced to resign his seat some time later after he was transferred outside Donegal by his employer, in circumstances which Sacks called 'suspicious'. Sacks also observed that while 'the circumstances surrounding this transaction are vague, if not obscure, that the Blaneys were the beneficiaries of this transaction is, however, quite clear'. A 'Blaneyite' was co-opted onto the Council in place of Harkin and those cumainn secretaries who had shown any support for Harkin were replaced by Blaney supporters.

With the loss of his ministerial post and his officer position within Fianna Fáil, Blaney was predicting an internal party challenge for his Dáil seat at the next general election, probably from his old rival Bernard McGlinchey. To ensure political survival Blaney increased his local involvement. He took positions on the Donegal Vocational Education Committee and the Board of the Letterkenny Regional Technical College. Nevertheless, the local Fianna Fáil organisation in the constituency was dividing for and against Blaney and it was only to be a matter of time before a split was to occur.

The role of Jim Gibbons in the whole Arms Crisis remains a matter of dispute. He said he played no part in the events leading up to and including the importation of arms in April 1970. Blaney says that Gibbons was involved and that when Albert Luykx and Captain James Kelly said that the arms importation was legal that they are correct. According to Gerry Jones, 'Right throughout the whole thing you had perfidy and double-standards. I remember Neil Blaney and I were sitting in the Parliamentary Secretaries' den one evening and Jim Gibbons came over and said "Neil – we're all in this together".' At the trial there was a direct contradiction between the evidence given by Charles Haughey and Jim Gibbons on the issue of a conversation concerning the attempted arms importation. This led Justice Henchy to say in his summing up remarks to the jury, 'There does not seem to me to be any way of avoiding the total conflict on this issue between Mr Haughey and Mr Gibbons'. The

Opposition parties pressed a confidence motion against Mr Gibbons as a man who misled the Dáil on the subject of the 1970 Arms Affair and sought to declare him unworthy of serving as a deputy and Minister.

Gibbons was, at this stage, in Blaney's old post of Agriculture, having been promoted by Lynch in the reshuffle which followed the dismissals of the previous year. The Government's majority in the Dáil was tight and only a handful of defections would have been enough to bring about a general election. All eyes focused upon former Ministers Charles Haughey and Neil Blaney and the direction they would vote in. Haughey and Blaney were faced with a dilemma. If they voted for the motion, or even abstained, they were guilty of supporting a Fine Gael motion which ultimately sought to undermine a Fianna Fáil Government. Such action would result possibly in banishment into the political wilderness. On the other hand, if they voted with Lynch and his Government they would be publicly supporting a man, Jim Gibbons, for whom they held nothing but contempt. Haughey chose to swallow his pride and voted, pragmatically, with the Government.

Neil Blaney, along with Paudge Brennan, abstained. In a short speech to a packed Dáil chamber and over-crowded public galleries, Blaney attacked Jim Gibbons. They were being asked, he said, to vote on Gibbons' actions, thereby saying that they did not believe he had misled the House or Courts. Thus they were being asked to say that what Gibbons did was right and what those who were prosecuted by the State did was wrong. 'The vote tonight called on me to say whether Mr Gibbons was telling the truth or that I was a liar.' He ended his speech with the words – 'That is what I am being asked to do, and that is what I am not prepared to do for anybody'.

When Blaney sat down he was cheered by the Opposition members and the public galleries. There was not, however, a cheer or a clap from the Fianna Fáil benches which listened in stony silence. Despite the abstentions of Blaney and Brennan, the Fianna Fáil Government survived the crucial no-confidence vote by 72 votes to 69. Blaney said afterwards that he had with great regret taken his decision to abstain. He spoke, however, of his determination to remain active in political life. The motivating forces behind his wish to stay in politics were both local and national. He said that in his constituency there were so many people whom he had, at that stage, represented for twenty-three years who did not want him to retire. Moreover, on the national scale, there were many thousands with beliefs similar to his own on Northern Ireland. 'I believe that any opting out by me from public life would be letting them down and letting the people of the Six Counties down,' Blaney said, as he added that, 'I have no intention of leaving the party unless the party leaves me'.

There were many who felt that Fianna Fáil had already left Neil Blaney. The battle for the soul of Fianna Fáil, which had begun in earnest with the election of Jack Lynch as leader and continued to simmer from the outbreak of the Troubles in the Six Counties, reached a head with the dismissals in May 1970. *The Irish Times*, the day after the Gibbons vote, used a headline – 'Blaney Tears his Career Apart'. It was totally accurate in terms of the former Minister's Fianna Fáil career. It was only a matter of time before the inevitable occurred and Jack Lynch moved to remove the Donegal man totally from the Fianna Fáil ranks.

Moves to expel the dissidents from the Fianna Fáil Parliamentary Party began almost immediately. At a press conference following the vote, Jack Lynch expressed his wish that the party whip be removed from Blaney and Brennan immediately. 'This was a crucial division and their abstention could have caused the Government to be defeated,' Lynch said. Importantly, he added that neither of the two would be ratified as candidates in the next general election. Support from the party's National Executive for the expulsion of Blaney from the Fianna Fáil organisation itself would have been forthcoming, should Lynch have sought it. However, at that stage the Taoiseach preferred to close ranks and preserve his Fianna Fáil Government which then had only 69 votes under the party whip, compared to a combined, although diverse, Opposition of 74 votes.

The Donegal North East Dáil Ceanntair backed Neil Blaney in his decision to abstain on the 'Gibbons motion'. They called on Lynch not to remove the party whip from their Dáil deputy. The Dungloe cumann, one of the strongest in the constituency, condemned any attempt to expel Blaney. In a statement it said, 'Neil Blaney has done far too much good to be rewarded with an expulsion ticket from the organisation which the Blaneys over the years have made such a massive contribution towards'. The statement concluded, ' In the interests of unity and progress, North and South, we have requested the Taoiseach not to withdraw the whip from our Donegal hero'.

Neil Blaney was not, however, a 'hero' in the eyes of the Taoiseach, who prompted a motion at the next Fianna Fáil parliamentary meeting to remove the whip from Neil Blaney and Paudge Brennan. The voting in favour of their expulsion from the Parliamentary Party was 58 while 8 deputies opposed the motion with three abstaining. Two others were excused: the Minister for Justice, Des O'Malley, who was speaking in the Dáil Chamber and his predecessor, Micheál O'Moráin. The meeting lasted approximately an hour and a half with little bitterness surfacing publicly. Blaney 'regretted' that he had to be expelled after twenty-three years in politics. He emphasised that he was still a member of the Fianna Fáil party and that he considered himself a Fianna Fáil member of the Dáil. He indicated that, despite his abstention on the no-confidence motion, his support would be fully behind the Government. He did, however, reserve his vote in relation to Northern Ireland and any further confidence motions on Jim Gibbons.

The following weekend at a meeting in Letterkenny, Neil Blaney was less restrained as he told about four hundred supporters who attended in heavy rain, 'Give shelter to those who come to you, give them aid and money and anything else that might be useful to them. Let the people who are carrying on the struggle in the Six Counties know that you are with them. This is a continuation of 1916 and 1921 and it never can be finished until the whole country is free'. Conor Cruise O'Brien has stated that, 'It may be safely assumed that Blaney, while in office, acted on these principles'. O'Brien, who was Minister for Posts and Telegraphs in the 1973-77 Fine Gael-Labour Coalition, does not hold Blaney in high esteem. 'Mr Blaney is a very forceful man indeed, with pale, piercing eyes, a blue spade-shaped chin and a deliberate, faintly menacing manner.'

On that night in Letterkenny, Blaney's car was met at the outskirts of the town and a guard of honour of his supporters marched on each side of it to the Market Square. There, he was carried shoulder high to the platform. He told his audience that his expulsion from the Parliamentary Party served only to expose the weakness of those left behind. His jeering of the Taoiseach may once have been threatening, but in November 1971 the reality was that Jack Lynch most certainly held the reins of power in Fianna Fáil.

Lynch's upper hand over the Fianna Fáil organisation was clearly evident at the 1972 Ard-Fheis. Blaney, Brennan and Des Foley, who had also been expelled from the Parliamentary Party, were all refused deputy's admission passes to the Ard-Fheis. Brennan and Foley did not attend, but Neil Blaney got an ordinary delegate's pass from his own comhairle ceanntair. When he raised the issue at the Ard-Fheis, Blaney warned that, as they had been refused deputy's admission passes, they would have to decide whether in future they should feel bound to support the Government in the Dáil. It was a threat which the delegates in the RDS, when the Ard Fheis opened, took lightly.

In many ways the 1972 Ard-Fheis signalled the final parting between Neil Blaney and the Fianna Fáil organisation. The Lynch faction was now dominant and totally in control. Throughout the country dissident members had been rooted out and, at all levels of the party structure, positions of responsibility were held by Lynch loyalists. It was these individuals who made up the overwhelming majority of delegates at the 1971 and 1972 Ard-Fheiseanna. There was loud applause at the 1972 Ard-Fheis for contributions from Paddy Hillery, George Colley and Lynch himself, whose entrance throughout the weekend brought the delegates to their feet. Jack Lynch and people of his mould were totally dominant in Fianna Fáil.

The mention of the name Neil Blaney in previous years would have induced a deafening response, more often then not, bringing delegates to their feet in thunderous applause. At the 1972 Ard-Fheis there was genuine applause for the man from Donegal, but it was far from the enthusiastic response of old. Indeed, on this occasion, jeers were heard alongside the cheers. John Healy, writing in *The Irish Times*, noted that, 'Even in his face, there was not the look of confidence that you remembered from other years and other tight moments.' It was to be, nevertheless, a fitting finale for Blaney. He took his place with the ordinary party members for the honour of addressing the Ard-Fheis platform. His introduction of himself still remains one of the most memorable lines of any Fianna Fáil Ard-Fheiseanna, since the Party foundation. 'My name is Blaney and I am representing Donegal North East,' were the words that the former Minister spat out as he asserted his right to address an Ard-Fheis that the party establishment had attempted to keep him away from. While he was given a big ovation, despite the catcalls, when he concluded his speech, his strongest applause came when he suggested a minute's silence for all those who had died in Northern Ireland.

The case of Neil Blaney was simmering, waiting to be finally addressed. This was particularly so given the determination of Jack Lynch that the Donegal deputy would not be a Fianna Fáil candidate at the next general election. There was, therefore, pressure on the Fianna Fáil leader to deal with Blaney. Matters were brought to a head by the divisions within the Fianna Fáil organisation in Donegal North East, which was split along pro- and anti-Blaney lines.

Attempts by Blaney and his supporters to organise the party's national collection independently in Donegal North East were seized upon by Lynch to finally address the issue.

On Monday 26 June 1972, Neil T. Blaney was expelled from the Fianna Fáil Party by 'an overwhelming majority' of the seventy-two member National Executive for 'conduct unbecoming for a member of the organisation'. Neil Blaney was now expelled from the entire Fianna Fáil organisation and all of its branches, including his own cumann in Donegal. It was said afterwards that the vote at the National Executive was 69 to 2, with one abstention. There was no representative from Donegal North East due to 'voting and procedural irregularities' in the election earlier that year. Blaney, who was no longer a member of the National Executive, had a letter read to the meeting asking to be allowed to address the Executive, so as to make a case against his dismissal. An amendment to the original motion to allow this to happen was, however, defeated.

It was left to Tommy Mullins, General Secretary of the party, to issue the short, curt statement which severed Blaney's connection with Fianna Fáil. The statement read: 'At a special meeting of the National Executive of Fianna Fáil tonight, it was decided to expel Mr Neil T. Blaney, T.D., from the Fianna Fáil organisation in accordance with Rule 7 of the party rules'. There was no mention of his service to the party, his achievements as the great organiser or his successes in the thirteen years spent as a Government Minister. The history of the man who was a candidate for leadership of the Party in 1966 was simply being erased by Fianna Fáil.

— 6 —
Outside, never to return

Neil Blaney found himself in the political wilderness in June 1972, stripped of all the trappings of party political and governmental power which had been his for so long. He says that he did not regret what had happened or miss the positions of influence he had held. He stood by his beliefs and that is all that matters. Nevertheless, no matter how much he denies it, he was bitterly disappointed and the rejection stung. These emotions are raised, and the guard drops, when he speaks of Jack Lynch. In one interview he said, 'I am still very angry about it because the question can still be asked – "Why was I dismissed?" and there is no answer to that, apart from the fact that I did not see eye to eye, then or since, with the Fianna Fáil establishment on the Six Counties'. When the *Magill* Arms Crisis issues were debated in the Dáil in late 1980 Lynch said, 'I want to say categorically that I did not . . . promise arms to people who came to me from the North', to which Blaney from across the Dáil Chamber replied, 'The deputy did not refuse them'.

Despite his parting with Fianna Fáil Neil Blaney continued to hold support in his Donegal constituency, as well as in numerous pockets throughout the country. Talk of his return to the party fold simmered after his expulsion in 1972. It came as no surprise then when a resolution recommending an invitation to the former Minister to return to Fianna Fáil came before the party's 1976 Ard-Fheis. The resolution was proposed by Dungarvan Comhairle Ceantair and had the backing of party units in Dingle, Maynooth, Clare and Waterford. Jack Lynch and his advisors decided in 1976 that the issue would have to be dealt with head-on. Replying to the resolution, the Fianna Fáil leader said that he strongly recommended the rejection of the motion because the party's interests would be seriously damaged if Deputy Blaney was to re-join. 'I believe that it would be seriously damaging to our party's interests if Deputy Blaney joined us as a result of this motion.' Lynch went on to say that he would reject Blaney's membership on two grounds: first, lack of loyalty and second due to Blaney's failure to subscribe to party policy on Northern Ireland.

Relations between Blaney and Lynch had not been helped by the fact that Blaney had embarrassed the Fianna Fáil leader in the Dáil debate on the Sunningdale Agreement in 1974. Blaney was an adamant critic of Sunningdale, which he believed did nothing to advance the cause of nationalists in Northern Ireland. James Downey has written that, 'Neil Blaney embarrassed Lynch by tabling a strongly anti-partition amendment to the Government motion of support for the agreement; and party opinion forced Lynch and his deputies to vote for the Blaney amendment instead of backing, as he would have wished, the Government line'.

Proposing the motion to invite Blaney to re-join the party, Robert Keane, a delegate from Waterford, said that the motivating reason for the motion was Blaney's continued assertion that he had not left Fianna Fáil but that the party had left him. Keane said that he had no reason to believe otherwise. He went on to record Blaney's sterling service to the party and country, and to outline his own opinion that the return of the man from Donegal would be only positive for Fianna Fáil. A delegate from Donegal addressed the issue with an emphatic reply –'The message from Donegal is "We don't want him".' Following loud applause, the Ard-Fheis overwhelmingly rejected the resolution by a show of hands. Interestingly, when the debate on the Blaney motion ended and the next subject was called about one third of the delegates left the main hall where the debates were taking place. In a response to the outcome of the debate, Neil Blaney accused Lynch of allowing the motion to be put on the Ard-Fheis clár so that it could be 'batted down in a stage-managed affair'. He added that Jack Lynch 'took the opportunity to do a Pontius Pilate in my absence so that, being the great democrat he purports to be, he could say that the decision had been taken by all the party'.

Along with talk of Neil Blaney's return to Fianna Fáil, at various stages throughout the period after his expulsion there has recurred periodic speculation that he was to launch a new national political party. The urgings for such a move generally stemmed from Blaney's supporters and friends rather than from the man himself who repeatedly kicked the idea to touch. Blaney could, in the early 1970s, have joined Kevin Boland in Aontacht Éireann. He had an open invitation to do so and indeed Boland left the position of party leader vacant to be filled by Haughey or Blaney, should either have joined. Following the Cabinet dismissals in May 1970, a united front from Haughey, Boland and Blaney, with the establishment of a new political party under their leadership may have challenged Fianna Fáil and totally changed Irish political life. Mutual mistrust between the three former Cabinet colleagues failed, however, to bring about such a development, and as the weeks and months from May 1970 passed, all hopes of the three men unifying behind any new party finally receded.

Haughey was to go silent and bide his time before returning to the top within Fianna Fáil. Blaney stayed in political life, but outside the Fianna Fáil fold. Boland attempted to challenge his old party's dominance with the establishment of Aontacht Éireann, which attracted over 1,000 people to its founding Ard Fheis. Neil Blaney, however, did not join. He had been elected to Dáil Eireann when the first Inter-Party Government was in power and he witnessed the demise of both Clann na Poblachta and Clann na Talmhan, two parties launched in the 1940s to challenge the established order. Aware of this experience, Blaney, ever the political realist, did not join Aontacht Éireann for the simple reason that he judged its chances of usurping Fianna Fáil's national power base as being slim. He watched Boland form his own political party and, having seen Clann na Poblachta's demise, he was not surprised by the electoral consequences for Aontacht Éireann. This political reality has guided his decisions on the establishment of a nationally based political organisation at all subsequent stages.

Following his 1979 European election success, Blaney's supporters were firmly behind the idea of launching a thirty-two county political party which would espouse the views that over 80,000 voters had backed in his election to the European Parliament. Certainly the case for the success of such a party was evident, with strong republican candidates having a chance of being elected in constituencies such as Cavan-Monaghan, Meath, Kerry South, Kerry North and Carlow-Kilkenny. In addition, the Irish Independent Party in Northern Ireland was attempting to persuade Blaney to launch any new political organisation on a thirty-two county basis. Several meetings of Blaney's supporters were held to discuss the idea, but in the end Blaney's personal reluctance killed off all such plans. The magnitude of the task was daunting. Blaney knew that being successful in certain areas was one thing, but it was a different ball-game to successfully launch a national challenge to the existing parties. Moreover, should any new party fail, like Clann na Poblachta or Aontacht Éireann, it was likely that those associated with it would be politically obliterated. Neil Blaney was not for undermining his Donegal seat in Dáil Eireann and having his political career ended in the fashion of others, like Seán Mac Bride and Kevin Boland who had both attempted to launch new political parties but saw their efforts fail to go the distance.

A mixture of factors combined to prevent Blaney returning to Fianna Fáil in the period after his expulsion in 1972. Most obvious were the differences in policy in relation to Northern Ireland. The individual political agenda of Lynch and Haughey, when in the position of party leader, were also contributing factors. Lynch's feelings towards the readmission of Blaney had been articulated very clearly at the 1976 Ard-Fheis, while Haughey was fearful of Blaney and he probably did not want within the party ranks so prominent a reminder of his silent past. More important factors, however, which prevented Blaney's return were the deep divisions and bitter resentments between his supporters and those who had stayed loyal to the party after the 1972 expulsion.

The Fianna Fáil organisation in Donegal North East and Donegal South West have repeatedly made clear their opposition to Neil Blaney's readmission to the party. Fighting each other with great rivalry at election times from the 1973 general election onwards had deepened the feelings of bitterness between the two sides. The success of Blaney's Independent Fianna Fáil organisation in the 1976 by-election in Donegal North East and the European Parliamentary election in 1979 only served to add to the bad blood. Indeed, the local Donegal Fianna Fáil organisation felt so strongly about the support given by the former Fianna Fáil deputy, Dr Paddy Delap, for Blaney's candidate, Paddy Kelly, in the February 1982 general election that they expelled Delap from the local organisation. Delap, who won a Dáil seat in a 1970 by-election before losing it in the 1973 general election, went on to join Independent Fianna Fáil and won a seat on Donegal County Council for Blaney's organisation in 1985.

The split necessitated a total revamping of the Fianna Fáil organisation in the constituency with a whole new cumainn structure being put in place by the party's headquarters. This reorganisation allowed scope for many individuals who had previously been unable to establish themselves in their own right, due to the Blaney dominance. Bernard McGlinchey was one of these individuals. With a base in Letterkenny, McGlinchey, a Senator since, was never going to be in a position to go forward for a Dáil seat as a Fianna Fáil candidate while Neil Blaney was the principal power in the constituency. While McGlinchey was, as Kevin Boland says, 'one of Blaney's loyal supporters,' his geographical location in Letterkenny put him in too close a position to Blaney territory. McGlinchey had Dáil ambitions. Prior to the 1969 general election, rumours abounded in Donegal that he was going to seek a nomination at the selection convention. Negotiations ensued in the backrooms until McGlinchey relented. He was appointed

Director of Elections for the constituency and arrived at the selection convention just as Blaney and Cunningham had been reselected. In his possession he had the election posters and canvass cards, ready for distribution to party members, with the names Blaney and Cunningham printed on them! With the departure of Blaney from Fianna Fáil, Bernard McGlinchey saw his opportunity to obtain, as it were, promotion from the Seanad to Dáil Eireann.

At an election rally in Letterkenny during the 1969 general election, Senator Bernard McGlinchey recalled the by-election in 1948 which first elected Neil Blaney, as he told a cheering crowd – 'There were two candidates, one a blood relative of my own, and the other a Fianna Fáil man, and I danced in the streets when the Fianna Fáil man won. Fianna Fáil is more important than any blood relative.' For McGlinchey, Fianna Fáil was more important than even Neil Blaney as he stayed with the party and today he says that he 'has no interest or nothing to say about Mr Blaney'. With Blaney gone, McGlinchey, who had been forced to wait on the sidelines for so long, was presented with an opportunity of gaining a seat in the Dáil at the expense of his old friend. It was a fact which Blaney was very much aware of. 'There was nothing very secure facing into the 1973 election,' Blaney remembers. His organisation was, however, strong enough to hold their man's seat in what was his first election campaign not running on the Fianna Fáil party ticket. The distribution of the seats in Donegal North East was then as it has continued to be – one Fianna Fáil, one Fine Gael and Neil Blaney.

Bernard McGlinchey had only been added to the ticket by the party's national executive after his failure to secure a nomination at the selection convention. Jack Lynch personally chaired the 1973 convention in Donegal North East and he backed Blaney's old rival John Harkin. Both Harkin and McGlinchey were, however, well beaten in the general election and neither was ever to win a Dáil seat. Neil Blaney's supporters were encouraged to cast only a single vote as a sign of their ill feelings towards Fianna Fáil to whom the majority of their transfers would have been expected to go. When

Neil Blaney's surplus was distributed, following his first count election, it was spread almost evenly between Fianna Fáil and Fine Gael. Their point had been made. Neil Blaney said after the 1973 result that his election workers and supporters had done a great day's work on behalf of the Republican ideals. 'I hope that the wrong leadership that has put us on two sides of the road may be corrected, so that it may truly represent the aspirations of all Irishmen that Ireland should be one and that Ireland should be free.'

The ramifications of the Blaney expulsion and its impact on the Fianna Fáil party organisation in Donegal were still being experienced after the February 1973 general election. Blaney's successful defence of his seat as an Independent candidate was a bitter blow to those who had remained within the Fianna Fáil ranks. In May of the same year, the Fianna Fáil National Executive expelled five of its councillors on Donegal County Council and three Donegal based Urban District Councillors. These elected representatives, including Harry Blaney, Michael Derry, Patrick Friel and James Larkin, had supported Neil Blaney in the 1973 election and they were to form the backbone of his own constituency organisation. One person who stayed with Fianna Fáil and refused to join with Blaney spoke of the need to 'demolish Blaneyism in Donegal'.

Neil Blaney's organisation uses the name Independent Fianna Fáil. Initially Fianna Fáil was concerned about the possible confusion for the electorate, in particular on ballot papers, if Blaney's organisation registered the name, and it sought legal advice. In any event Neil Blaney has never registered Independent Fianna Fáil as a political party. The structure of Blaney's organisation is similar to Fianna Fáil's with cumainn throughout Donegal North East where his own power-base largely lies. Nevertheless, Blaney's successes in the 1979 and 1989 European elections have proved that support for the principles backed by Independent Fianna Fáil is found outside its home base. The organisation has councillors on several local authorities in border counties. Independent Fianna Fáil is active on Donegal County Council, which caters for all of Donegal County, and in the most recent Local Government elections in 1991 it won four seats. Harry Blaney leads the Independent Fianna Fáil group on the Council. After the 1991 local elections they signed a pact with Fine Gael and Fianna Fáil which will last for the lifetime of the present Council and divides the chairpersonship and membership of the Council and its sub-committees between the three parties.

Those involved in Independent Fianna Fáil see more, however, to the organisation than Neil Blaney. It would be wrong to see their allegiance as tied up with a Blaney personality-cult. These people share his political beliefs, which are fundamentally rooted in the question of the Border. Yet, as one political figure has remarked, 'Today, Blaney is a symbol more than a leader of Independent Fianna Fáil'. His supporters are not afraid to challenge the Blaneys, as they did when deciding who should be the MEP substitutes for Blaney in the event of his retiring. The Blaneys sought to have one of Neil Blaney's sons as the principal substitute, but the Independent Fianna Fáil organisation baulked at this proposal. Instead, Patrick Lenihan, a brother of Brian Lenihan and Mary O'Rourke, was selected as Blaney's substitute. Nevertheless, Neil Blaney has a tremendous capacity to motivate these people. His attitude is, 'Give your total commitment, otherwise give nothing'. The majority give, as they have given for many a long year, their total commitment. It has been said that Blaney does not ask for support, he simply expects it. It is this type of almost demanding arrogance which brought Fianna Fáil such electoral success throughout the 1960s as Blaney laid claim to the title of 'Great Organiser'. A typical Blaney speech demanded of his election workers during one campaign – 'Work to the last minute of the last hour to get those ballots in the box. Not one single one of you allow one single voter at one single polling station to slip away in the belief that we're home and dry'.

The result of the 1976 Donegal North East by-election was one of the early electoral successes for Blaney's Independent Fianna Fáil and an election Neil Blaney recalls fondly because of the result, but bitterly due to subsequent events. Liam Cunningham, who had been Blaney's Fianna Fáil running mate until they fought on different sides at the 1973 general election, died in 1976. There was speculation that the bad blood between Blaney and Bernard McGlinchey would mean that Blaney's organisation would contest the resulting by-election only if Bernard McGlinchey was the Fianna Fáil standard-bearer. A by-election win for McGlinchey would create an unwelcome political rival for Blaney in his own political patch at the following general election. Blaney was quick, however, to end such rumours. 'I am not a man for bitterness. I bear no ill-will, and even if I did, I would not make it a vehicle on which to ride into a by-election. If I am to be in, it will be through conviction, in accordance with principle and policy; and I'll be in to win, a feat which I don't consider impossible knowing as I do the feeling in the constituency.' In a selection convention conducted amid intense in-fighting, McGlinchey was beaten for the Fianna Fáil nomination, but regardless of the selection of Hugh Conaghan for Fianna Fáil, a 'Blaneyite' was proposed. This made the by-election a three way contest between Fianna Fáil, Fine Gael, Paddy Keavney of Independent Fianna Fáil, with a fourth candidate, an Independent, given little chance.

Independent Fianna Fáil ran a well organised campaign but, with the political heavyweights of Fianna Fáil and Fine Gael all drafted into the constituency for the duration of the campaign, Blaney was pensive prior to voting saying only that, 'We await the verdict of the people of North East Donegal with confidence'. He realised that the result would be close and, in fact, there was little between the three main candidates on the first count, with Paddy Keavney running second to Fine Gael's Joachim Loughrey, later to become a Senator, and Conaghan placed third. Despite a full recount, on the request of Fianna Fáil, little changed and with the distribution of the Independent candidate's votes, it became clear that the seat was between Fine Gael and Paddy Keavney. Conaghan was beaten and, with his transferable votes going almost two to one in favour of Paddy Keavney, Independent Fianna Fáil took the seat. When the returning officer announced the result there was near pandemonium in the count centre. Paddy Keavney and his Director of Elections, Neil Blaney, were carried shoulder high around the hall amid cries of 'Blaney for Taoiseach' and 'Lynch Out'.

It was, however, a short lived success. At the following general election, twelve months later, Keavney polled poorly and lost his seat in the newly formed Donegal five seat constituency to Fianna Fáil by-election candidate, Hugh Conaghan. Keavney remained a Donegal County Councillor for the party until he defected to Fianna Fáil in the run-up to the 1989 general election. He fought on a Fianna Fáil ticket in the most recent local elections in 1991 and held his seat, thus reducing Independent Fianna Fáil's total representation on the Council by one – to four seats. Keavney says he rejoined Fianna Fáil 'because they invited me back'. Blaney today ends dismissively any discussion of Keavney, a Moville undertaker, who he obviously feels let his organisation down.

The Fianna Fáil victory in the election of June 1977 was overwhelming, giving the party the biggest overall majority in Dáil Éireann since 1923. Neil Blaney argues that the election outcome was more a total rejection by the electorate of the outgoing Fine Gael-Labour coalition than an endorsement of Jack Lynch's Fianna Fáil. Such an analysis is, however, only partially true, as there can be no denying the high esteem that Lynch was held in throughout the country. Added to Lynch's personal appeal was the fact that the 1977 election campaign was organisationally probably one of Fianna Fáil's finest. The first two years of the Government's term were solid, but from mid-1979 the size of the Government's majority became its unravelling. Embarrassing U-turns on policy, a deteriorating economic situation and the poor outcome in the June European Parliamentary election all combined to put pressure on

Jack Lynch's leadership. He had decided that he would step down as Fianna Fáil leader and Taoiseach early in 1980. With his continued leadership perceived as a liability by Fianna Fáil back-benchers fearing for their Dáil seats, Jack Lynch was forced to bring his retirement back to early December 1979.

In almost a re-run of the 1966 leadership election, Charles Haughey and George Colley lined up to succeed Jack Lynch. The only difference with thirteen years earlier was that Neil Blaney now stood on the side-lines, without any influence over the outcome. Looking back, Brian Lenihan believes that, 'If Blaney had put his head down and gone along with Lynch in that period 1968-69 and stayed with that into the '70s, then he could never have been caught'. Watching from the outside, from Neil Blaney's perspective the election of Haughey was the obvious preferred result. Whatever about the genuineness of Haughey's republicanism, Blaney knew that George Colley's views on Northern Ireland would not coincide with his own. When Charles Haughey narrowly defeated George Colley for the leadership of Fianna Fáil in December 1979, talk of Blaney's return once again grew. Men like Paudge Brennan and Seán Sherwin who had split with the party over Lynch's line on Northern Ireland re-joined, in anticipation of a return to a more republican ethos in Fianna Fáil now that Haughey was leader.

Neil Blaney was in the United States at the time and he congratulated Haughey by phone on his election as Taoiseach and Fianna Fáil leader. Speaking in Sligo in January 1980, Blaney said that there was no question of him reapplying for membership of Fianna Fáil unless the Government changed its policy in relation to Northern Ireland. He said he would await the response of Haughey when the Dáil reassembled after the Christmas recess and also at the forthcoming Ard-Fheis. While Neil Blaney won many concessions from Haughey, ultimately Fianna Fáil's policy on Northern Ireland changed little throughout the entire period of Haughey's leadership. 'Haughey himself turned out to be more Lynch-like than Jack Lynch himself,' Blaney now says.

Charlie Haughey, he now believes, was a 'republican while it was in fashion and wasn't when it went out of fashion'. Blaney's feelings towards his one-time Cabinet colleague are laced with both sadness and bitterness. It is the sadness that dominates. 'It took me thirty years to find out that he was no friend,' Blaney says, recalling how he used to fly in to Dublin from the European Parliament in Strasburg by special plane, at his own expense, so as to vote for the 1982 minority Haughey Government. 'I wouldn't do it now, even if I was still supporting him,' he adds. In October 1982, in a confidence debate on Haughey's minority Government which had been dogged by misfortune and was to lead to the creation of the term 'GUBU', Blaney explained why he was supporting Haughey – 'I am not satisfied with Charlie Haughey and I have told him so. But on the national question, he is at least by far the best we have available from any side of the House'. Bruce Arnold, who has watched the relationship between the two men since the early 1960s, argues that Blaney was always aware of the shallowness of Haughey's beliefs on Northern Ireland and that he only supported Haughey because Haughey was in a sense 'the lesser of two evils'. Arnold adds that, 'Blaney knew from 1960 to 1969 the kind of person Charles Haughey was, a non-republican, Lemass-type clone who was interested in economics and would have shown little genuine interest in Northern Ireland. Haughey was Blaney's best chance of getting republican views high-up on the agenda in mainstream politics'.

According to Gerry Jones, who worked with both men, 'Charlie wept on his (Blaney's) shoulder a few times. Neil was always available to go up to Kinsealy. Haughey knew that Neil had a very clear view of events and was pretty good at the prognosis'. Neil Blaney says of his friendship with Haughey – 'I was his friend right up the years. It took me until the mid-1980s to realise that Charlie was all take, so that we were never really friends. I just thought we were'. They had known each other since the mid-1950s when they were both members of the Fianna Fáil National Executive. Yet, despite this, the relationship between Haughey and Blaney is probably best described as a political relationship. They may have respected each other, but it would appear that there was always prevalent a sense of deep mistrust. This is clearly evident through events such as the 1966 leadership contest and the Arms Crisis. When Haughey came to power in late 1979, nothing had changed and this pattern of distrust was evident very early in Haughey's term as Fianna Fáil leader. Blaney wrote to Haughey during the 1980-81 hunger strikes asking him to put more pressure on the British Prime Minister, Margaret Thatcher, to make concessions to end the strikes. Blaney has admitted that he received no acknowledgement of this correspondence. In addition, after Blaney, Dr John O'Connell and Síle de Valera met with Bobby Sands during his hunger strike in Long Kesh, Haughey held meetings with O'Connell and de Valera, but pointedly he had no meeting with Blaney.

Indeed, it would seem that in the period from December 1979 until June 1981 there was no formal contact between the two men and when contact was made, in June 1981, it was only when it was politically expedient to do so, to secure Blaney's vote for Haughey in the election of Taoiseach. Ironically, Charles Haughey's first election test as leader of Fianna Fáil came in October 1980 in Donegal. The by-election was due to the death of the Ceann Comhairle, Joe Brennan, and was fought in the then five seat constituency which encompassed all of County Donegal. At the Independent Fianna Fáil selection convention, Blaney laid his cards very much on the table when he declared that there was little to choose on Northern Ireland policy between Charles Haughey and Jack Lynch. Fianna Fáil was, however, leaving nothing to chance and was going all out to ensure that a repeat of the 1976 by-election win for Blaney was not going to occur. Given that the campaign was fought over the entire county of Donegal, Blaney's strength was inevitably going to be diluted, but as Stephen O'Byrnes has written: 'For the three weeks before voting, the entire Government decamped to furthest Donegal. Haughey spent five weekends there, and the vote-catching promises were flung about the country like snuff at a wake'. During one of these visits Haughey spoke of Blaney as a 'sean cara' and there was talk in the constituency that the effort of the Blaney machine was been tuned down because Blaney was seeking to return to Fianna Fáil. Blaney was, however, quick to scotch these rumours and it is said that on the last weekend before polling day, he attained a record seven after-Mass speeches between 9.00 a.m. and 11.30 a.m. This commitment was not to take the seat as, to Blaney's disappointment, the Fianna Fáil candidate won.

Charles Haughey called a general election in June 1981, but the outcome led to Fianna Fáil's loss of office to a coalition administration led by Garret FitzGerald. Blaney supported Haughey in the vote for Taoiseach, but this support was in vain as Fianna Fáil was several seats short of a majority. This Fine Gael-Labour Coalition was itself, however, short of a Dáil majority and it fell seven months later in January 1982. Many in Fianna Fáil were of the opinion that a minority Fianna Fáil Government could be formed without need for a general election. Under the Constitution, the President has the right to refuse a dissolution of the Dáil to a Taoiseach who has lost a confidence motion. In such an event, the President would be expected to call on the leader of a group who might be in a position to put together a Government that could win the confidence of the majority of Dáil deputies. The FitzGerald led coalition fell at 8.00 p.m. and in the two hour period before the Fine Gael leader made his way to Áras an Uachtaráin to request the then President, Paddy Hillery, to dissolve the Dáil, senior Fianna Fáil figures attempted to ascertain if they could form a Government without the need for a general election. As early as twenty minutes after the Coalition Government fell, Fianna Fáil released a statement saying that Charlie Haughey was available for consultation with the President should he so wish. The support of a number of Independent TDs was going to be vital if such a plan was to come off. With this situation in mind Neil Blaney was approached to see if he would support any minority Fianna Fáil administration. He met with Haughey and the question of Hillery refusing Garrett FitzGerald's request and calling on Haughey to form a Government was discussed. Blaney was favourably disposed to supporting Haughey, but the plan unravelled because Paddy Hillery was furious at the pressure applied to him and he dissolved the Dáil after meeting with Garrett FitzGerald. These events of January 1982 were to assume a vital significance during the 1990 Presidential election.

An overall majority once again eluded Fianna Fáil in the February 1982 general election and Haughey found himself needing the support of Independents to form a Government. A six man delegation from Independent Fianna Fáil met with Haughey to discuss the terms for Neil Blaney's support. His vote was conditional upon a tougher stance by Haughey on Northern Ireland and an incentive package for the construction industry to generate employment. Since the election Haughey had been telling Blaney, in private, that their views on the North coincided and that they were following similar agenda. Blaney now wanted these utterances made public. Without his agreement on this the delegation told Haughey, their man would abstain on the vote for his election as Taoiseach. Haughey knew that such action would be enough to deprive him of the position and agreed to the demands of Blaney and his delegation. In a similar way Haughey bought the support of Tony Gregory, with a promised massive investment deal for Dublin's inner city areas. With such support from Independents and the three Sinn Féin – The Workers' Party deputies Haughey was, in fact, elected Taoiseach, in what was to be his short lived administration of 1982. In his acceptance speech Haughey told the Dáil that the new Government would seek 'the final withdrawal of the British military and political presence' from Northern Ireland. Blaney had got his way although, as he was to realise over the following years, Haughey could use the 'green card' on occasions to suit his needs without any substantial follow-up on his words. The promised investment injection for the construction industry, however, never materialised.

At the same meeting Neil Blaney also got a separate agreement from Haughey to appoint one of his supporters to the Seanad, as one of the Taoiseach's eleven nominees. In return, Blaney promised the support of his followers for Fianna Fáil candidates on all Seanad election panels. The deal was based on Blaney's belief that he could deliver 28 votes in the Seanad election from county councillors throughout the country, which was enough, if the votes were cast strategically, to determine the outcome of at least one Seanad seat. The agreement was Blaney at his political best. He told Haughey that without this support Fianna Fáil was unlikely, even with the Taoiseach's eleven nominated Senators, to achieve more that thirty of the sixty seats in the Seanad. In such an event a new minority Fianna Fáil Government faced a tough time in the Upper House.

Haughey saw the political reality of Blaney's proposition and agreement was reached. With the help of Blaney's promised votes Fianna Fáil won an extra Seanad seat, while Haughey subsequently appointed James Larkin, Blaney's Director of Elections, to the Seanad. Blaney was later proved totally correct in his reading of the situation. In the Seanad election which followed the fall of Haughey's Government in November 1982, Larkin ran as an Independent Fianna Fáil candidate and received 30 votes, two more than Blaney's initial estimate of the support he could rely on. The appointment of a 'Blaneyite' to the Seanad was met with intense hostility by the Fianna Fáil organisation in Donegal, although the resentment was eased a little by the fact that also among Haughey's eleven nominees was Bernard McGlinchey, who had lost his Seanad seat in the most recent election. Nevertheless, the Donegal North East Dáil Cheantair passed motions which expressed its total disagreement with the appointment of James Larkin, while it also called on the Taoiseach to refute any alleged deals with Independent Fianna Fáil and to cease all further discussions with them. Furthermore, it was unanimously decided that the Donegal North East was 'totally opposed to any return of Neil Blaney to the Fianna Fáil Party'.

Added to these expressions of disquiet in Donegal Charlie Haughey had other, potentially more damaging, revolts to worry him. Haughey's victory over George Colley in 1979 had never been fully accepted by a large segment of the party. It was, therefore, no surprise that after electoral disappointment and embarrassing Government scandals, Haughey's leadership of Fianna Fáil came continuously under threat in the period between 1981 and 1983. Neil Blaney had hard words to say about Dessie O'Malley and the others involved in the anti-Haughey faction. In Blaney's opinion they were being disloyal to the leadership of Fianna Fáil, regardless of their own personal views on the individual who held that position. He asked – 'Are these people democrats and, if so, do they agree to accept a majority decision? If they are not prepared to accept that, then there is no place for them in political power in this country'.

During the third challenge to Haughey's leadership in early 1983, when it looked as if he was going to resign, some of Haughey's staunchest supporters approached Blaney in an attempt to get him to persuade Haughey to fight the challenge. Neil Blaney says that he was instrumental in kick-starting Haughey's political career. 'I encouraged Charlie Haughey into his success in politics. I would have been largely instrumental in his first appointment by his father-in-law Seán Lemass.' Blaney tells of how Haughey was one of the people considered for promotion when a vacancy became available for a Parliamentary Secretary (similar to Minister for State) in Lemass's Government in 1960. 'It took a lot of convincing, to get Lemass to agree.' Now, over twenty years later, Blaney was again supportive of the man he had backed when he first came into politics. Blaney spoke with Haughey by phone and told him it was his responsibility to both party and country to remain as leader. The conversation clearly showed that a little Fianna Fáil blood still remained in Blaney's veins as he argued with Haughey that without an obvious successor, the likelihood was the permanent internal division of Fianna Fáil into numerous impotent factions. Charlie Haughey did not, in fact, resign and he went on to lead Fianna Fáil for another nine years. Blaney claims that while Haughey may now deny his role, he did, in fact, stop Haughey from resigning. 'He, effectively, had resigned. The resignation was written out.' Looking back over Haughey's political career Blaney now says, 'I helped him to survive in his worst days. I helped him to survive even when he was at the top'.

In July 1982, Dr Bill Loughnane, a colourful Clare deputy with strong republican convictions, suggested that Blaney be readmitted to Fianna Fáil. The idea provoked outright opposition from George Colley, Jim Gibbons and many Fianna Fáil people in Donegal North East. Nevertheless, the 'Blaney question' continued to simmer within grassroot Fianna Fáil circles, with many seeing the return of the Donegal man as an ideal response to the manoeuvres of the Colley/O'Malley faction. It seems that Haughey was not of this view, given his reaction to calls at the 1983 Ard-Fheis for Blaney's readmission. Haughey's leadership had been under threat over the previous twelve months and, while he had relied on Blaney's advice to overcome these threats, the last thing he needed in early 1983 was the issue of Blaney's readmission adding to his detractors' ammunition and rekindling the leadership issue. The Kilkenny Comhairle Dáil Ceanntair were the principal sponsors of this potentially explosive resolution at the 1983 Ard-Fheis, where at least fifteen similar motions were received for inclusion on the clár. The motion asked that the Donegal Fianna Fáil organisation be requested to consider the readmission of Blaney. For many in the party, however, the issue came too soon after the turmoil of the previous year and the timing was considered to be politically inopportune. With these arguments to the fore the motion was withdrawn, following a meeting on the Saturday night of the Ard-Fheis between their sponsors, the party chairman Jim Tunney and Haughey himself. Nevertheless, hundreds of delegates still stood to applaud and chant, 'We Want Blaney'.

In early 1983 Charlie Haughey had good personal reasons for keeping Neil Blaney on the margins and not embracing him back into Fianna Fáil. There still remained a fear that Blaney could potentially represent a threat to his own leadership of the party either indirectly, by causing a challenge from the O'Malley/Colley faction which would strongly oppose any proposal for Blaney's return, or directly, through a challenge by Blaney himself for the leadership of the party, although this was itself highly unlikely. Nevertheless, the issue of Blaney's return was not going to go away that easily. With the expulsion of Des O'Malley, the environment was becoming more favourable for Blaney's return. Haughey was far more firmly in control of Fianna Fáil and many felt that it was now only a matter of time before Blaney was back within the fold. In addition, Fianna Fáil's adoption of a hardline stance in relation to Northern Ireland while in opposition during the 1982-87 period, helped to further reduce any differences between the party and Neil Blaney. Haughey had strongly argued that a unitary state was the only solution to the Northern problem and had rejected the other options suggested in the *New Ireland Forum Report* when it was published in May 1984. Haughey also denounced the Anglo-Irish Agreement when it was signed in November 1984 and under his leadership Fianna Fáil in opposition vigorously opposed extradition. This hard-line stance was, however, ultimately proved to be opportunistic and lacking in any genuine semblance of conviction.

Speculation that Blaney was on his way back was heightened when he attended an official Fianna Fáil function in Kilkenny. He had been invited to a ceremony to unveil a memorial to Eamon de Valera in Kilkenny and he used the event to indirectly attack Dessie O'Malley and his newly formed Progressive Democrats, the party the Limerick East deputy launched after his expulsion from Fianna Fáil. In the period after his expulsion, prior to the establishment of the Progressive Democrats, O'Malley sat with Blaney on the Independent benches in Dáil Eireann. O'Malley's supporters had taken to claiming that their fledgling party and its founding leader were 'breaking the mould in Irish politics'. Blaney, in his speech, emphatically told his Fianna Fáil audience that Eamon de Valera alone was the only mould breaker in Irish politics this century. Blaney had little time for the PDs and he accused O'Malley of 'reprehensible revisionism' and 'calculated disrespect to those involved on either side of the Civil War'. Des O'Malley has himself scant regard for 'civil war politics' which he considers to have little relevance to contemporary Ireland. 'Blaney never developed his views at all. I'd say he probably has much the same views today as he had thirty or forty years ago. That's the tragedy of the man. Blaney's obsessed with the past.' By criticising O'Malley and the Progressive Democrats Blaney was, however, endearing himself to the Fianna Fáil faithful for whom O'Malley and his new party were hate objects.

Again, prior to the 1985 Ard-Fheis, the issue of Blaney's return to Fianna Fáil arose with an invitation from his local cumann in Rossnakill in Fanad to re-join. The party establishment reacted quickly to kill any debate on the issue. The then General Secretary of Fianna Fáil, Frank Wall, was adamant that Blaney himself had to reapply for membership – 'If a person wishes to re-join, they must apply in the normal way and the application will be considered accordingly'. It was enough of a stumbling block for Neil Blaney who was not interested in pursuing an individual application for membership to a party which he still makes clear he never left. 'Let's make it quite clear: I was fired out of Fianna Fáil. I was fired as a Minister. I was charged as a conspirator. I was not returned for trial as distinct from my four co-accused. I was retained as "guilty" even though I wasn't tried. I was then, by connivance, counted out as a teller in charge of the election for Joint National Treasurer of Fianna Fáil. They took the party whip from me and then I was finally removed from the Fianna Fáil organisation and it took them two years to do it. Talk about a limpet on a rock, nothing was harder to shift out of Fianna Fáil than I was.'

In addition, Blaney no longer saw his return to Fianna Fáil on an individual basis; he was now the leader of a two to three thousand strong organisation which would collectively be joining with Fianna

Fáil. In May 1985, at the height of the speculation of his return, Blaney spelt out his thinking on the matter in a *Magill* interview with Olivia O'Leary.

'There are no rules in Fianna Fáil for the admission of an organisation. How can you put a two or three thousand member organisation into another organisation under rules which were drawn up for the admission of individuals into a local cumann? It has to be that everybody who would be associated with me in the organisation in Donegal, and outside of it, would be found their rightful place in the new scheme of things. Only that way will it work.'

Blaney was not returning to the party he had been expelled from in 1972 with cap in hand. A proud man, Neil Blaney was adamant that he was only going to return, walking tall, with his supporters alongside him. Nevertheless, the question of applying for membership or an amalgamation was not an insurmountable obstacle. Sustained efforts towards a reconciliation were underway in the 1985-86 period. In October 1985, an official approach was made by Independent Fianna Fáil directly to Charles Haughey, in order to finally end all the speculation and bring the two sides together. A letter signed by David McGuinness and Brian Gallagher, Chairman and Secretary of Independent Fianna Fáil respectively, requested a meeting 'to discuss the amalgamation of our respective Organisations'. It is highly unlikely that either man would have signed such a letter without the endorsement and approval of their party leader, Neil Blaney. The letter reads:

'Dear Mr Haughey,

Over the years and in particular during the past twelve months, there is evidence of a persistent and widespread demand that our two parties reconcile their differences in the interests of our Country.

Your recent statements on major policy matters and on the National issues in particular shows no significant differences from our party's point of view.

The support of our Organisation for you when in Government and at other crucial times has been consistent, even when to our detriment. The co-operation between our parties during the recent Local Elections campaign, and since, has resulted in our parties jointly taking control of all the elected bodies and their committees in counties Leitrim, Roscommon and Donegal.

We therefore request that you meet with a delegation from our party to discuss the amalgamation of our respective Organisations and have the matter resolved one way or the other.

If you accede to this request, we suggest that the meeting be held at the earliest possible date, and before the run-up to your next Ard Fheis commences.

Despite these sustained efforts towards reconciliation in the mid-1980s the amalgamation of the Independent Fianna Fáil organisation into Fianna Fáil itself never occurred, which Blaney now feels was due to the wishes of Charles Haughey. Indeed, traces of suspicion of Haughey's actual intentions can be found in the letter of October 1985 in which Blaney's supporters seek to have 'the matter resolved one way or the other'. Blaney now admits that 'Charlie Haughey was the person who didn't want me back in Fianna Fáil'. He goes on to say that – 'I do believe that, in a sense, Charlie was almost afraid of me as a personality who was very close to him, who had helped him so much. There was no question of his having to vie with me, I didn't want the top and never did and that I made quite clear; even on the day I declared as a would-be runner (in 1966) it was totally tactical'. In addition to the fear of a Blaney challenge to his leadership, however unlikely such an event, Haughey had other reasons for not favouring the return of Blaney. Haughey repeatly refused to discuss the events of 1969-1970. Blaney's readmission to Fianna Fáil would have meant the return of a constant reminder of a past which Haughey sought to erase. There was also the fear that in more urban areas like Dublin, the return of Blaney would be electorally damaging. As Gerald Barry wrote in *The Sunday Tribune* in 1985, 'There is the unuttered fear of what might be said one evening from the back of a lorry in Letterkenny'.

Brian Lenihan recalls the manoeuvres of the mid-1980s when it seemed as if Neil Blaney was returning. 'Charlie Haughey used his own political judgement. He had to look at the Fianna Fáil Party in the country as a whole . . . He had to present the party as a balanced national party, pursuing the middle ground. Charlie Haughey in his wisdom at that time didn't bring Blaney into the fold. I personally was in favour of it. I thought it would have been much better to have it done but it wasn't done.' Neil Blaney now admits that Haughey simply did not want either himself or his organisation. Many of Blaney's supporters feel that Haughey treated them poorly. Blaney himself says, 'We sought nothing from him, only the support we had given him and we were treated badly, shabbily and discourteously'.

By 1987 his contempt with the leadership of Charles Haughey was complete, largely due to the U-turns which Fianna Fáil made on extradition and the Anglo-Irish Agreement after they returned to Government in 1987. 'In 1985 the whole party, as articulated by Charlie Haughey, came out and shammed the Anglo-Irish Agreement left, right and centre, declaring that it copper-fastened partition. I clearly agreed then and I still agree, and I can't stand the idea that he operated it despite that.' Blaney was further embittered by Haughey's U-turn in relation to extradition between Ireland and the United Kingdom. In opposition, Fianna Fáil had vocally opposed extradition, but when in government after 1987, as Blaney says, extradition was 'Bloody well embraced by Fianna Fáil'. These U-turns on policy are to Neil Blaney not only examples of the loss of the traditional republican soul of the party, to which both his father and himself belonged, they also represent Haughey's lust for power. In early 1990 Blaney said, 'Every U-turn he's done has been aimed at him retaining that top spot. That's what makes the man tick'.

Neil Blaney says now that he feels only sadness when thinking of Haughey. 'He was power-mad. I don't have any doubt about that. It took me thirty years to find out that he was no friend. He was simply power-crazy with an ambition to be powerful for the power of position.' How else, Blaney asks, could 'Charlie have joined with Dessie in 1989 if it wasn't for his craze for power'? It was Neil Blaney who advised Charlie Haughey on his first property purchase and who brought him into the parade ring the first time he ever owned a racehorse. Yet of Haughey's retirement as Taoiseach and leader of Fianna Fáil in 1992 Blaney just says – 'What a pity he ever happened'.

— 7 —
Into Europe

'The European election campaign was tremendously hard work. In just thirty-six days, Neil covered 13,500 miles, walking approximately 150 of those with an average of three hours sleep a night' – so Eva Blaney describes her husband's 1979 campaign for the European Parliament. For all the political parties and their candidates it is a gruelling campaign; for an Independent candidate like Neil Blaney without the backing of a well spread organisation, the exercise is much more demanding. In 1979 his Euro-constituency, Connaught-Ulster, was extended over a large, eight county region, with an electorate of 437,000.

With Blaney's hat in the ring, Fianna Fáil knew that they were going to have an extremely hard task to take two of the three seats in Connaught-Ulster and an overall majority of the fifteen Irish seats in the European Parliament. Blaney's electoral strategy was evident from the outset of the campaign. He would play down his differences with Fianna Fáil and Jack Lynch, while at the same time projecting himself as the only true republican candidate on offer to the electorate. At the press conference to launch his campaign, he said that the real differences between himself and Fianna Fáil 'were largely disappearing'. He admitted that there existed a personality clash between himself and Jack Lynch, although he said he did not regard it as a difference that would separate him from the party. 'It is an obstacle but not an insuperable one,' Blaney stated as he went on to add that, 'There is no other republican voice, north or south, in this election.'

Neil Blaney was confident. He was assured of strong support in Donegal and he believed that there would be widespread backing for him elsewhere in his Euro-constituency. To many Fianna Fáil members in the west of Ireland, the Donegal man was still a 'Fianna

Fáiler', if very much on the fringe of the party. He was therefore likely to tap into the increasing disillusionment with the leadership of Jack Lynch. His wife canvassed in her native Mayo, while other members of his extended family and Independent Fianna Fáil machine took to the roads of Connaught-Ulster to get those all important number ones. Eva Blaney has been with Blaney throughout all the triumphs and disappointments of his political career. At the time of the 1979 election she said, 'Neil and I are very close, and we have discussed all his major decisions'.

They married in 1959. She is one of eight children from Mayo where her father, Michael Corduff, was a well-known collector of folklore. She trained as a nurse in the Mater Hospital and subsequently worked in Scotland as a midwife. 'During this time, my best friend was Neil's sister and it was through her that I came to know the Blaney family and Neil,' she says. Upon her return to Ireland, she was appointed a public nurse in Fanad. Eamon de Valera, then President of Ireland, attended their wedding, as did the Taoiseach Seán Lemass and future Taoisigh Jack Lynch and Charles Haughey and future Presidents Erskine Childers and Paddy Hillery. When one of his sons was born in 1966 Blaney announced it in the Dáil Chamber. He was passed a note which he read to himself and then turned the paper face downwards on the desk and smiled. The leader of the Labour Party, Brendan Corish, challenged him to read the note. In his dry Donegal way Blaney announced – 'It's a boy,' before adding, 'I have already put his name down on the housing list'. In the period after Blaney's dismissal from Cabinet they expanded the family farm which now stands at around 200 acres and opened the Milford Inn, among other ventures. They have five sons and two daughters, all of whom were old enough to lend a hand in the 1979 campaign.

Throughout the length and breath of Connaught-Ulster, Blaney supporters canvassed with their slogan, 'Send Blaney to Europe'. No stone was unturned in the effort to secure votes. The election coincided with the national postal strike in the Republic which closed off overseas canvassing. Unperturbed, Blaney placed an advertisement in *The Irish Post* in England, asking Irish emigrants for their support and for them to canvass their families at home on his behalf. A postal delivery service was offered by the Blaney election campaign from an address which they organised in County Tyrone in Northern Ireland.

Blaney is given to saying that his viewpoint is not just confined to Donegal but that it has solid support throughout all of Ireland. In 1979, the European Parliamentary election was, in many ways, a test of this opinion. Paudge Brennan, former Parliamentary Secretary at the Department of Local Government, was Blaney's Director of Elections. Brennan had resigned along with his Senior Minister, Kevin Boland, in protest against the dismissal of Haughey and Blaney in 1970. His father had been a Fianna Fáil TD for Wicklow and Brennan himself represented the constituency from 1954 until the 1973 general election when, disillusioned with Jack Lynch's leadership, he unsuccessfully contested the 1973 election as an Independent. Unlike Blaney, Paudge Brennan was to return to Fianna Fáil when Charles Haughey was elected leader in December 1979 and he was again a Dáil deputy for Wicklow from June 1981 to February 1982. At the end of the campaign, at a rally in Sligo, Brennan was thanked by Neil Blaney who said, 'My good friend and colleague, the son of a friend and colleague of my father, not just in elections, but in the prison camps'. It was as much a private apology as a public tribute, observed Gene Kerrigan, who followed the Blaney campaign in 1979. Blaney's 'apology' resulted from an incident in the dying hours of the 1979 campaign when he had 'had words' with Paudge Brennan, after he found out that his Director of Elections had neglected to arrange passes for Blaney's observers at polling booths, as well as designing posters which purported to be a 'specimen ballot paper' and which had to be altered before they could be used. Those who have worked in election campaigns with Neil Blaney know that he does not suffer fools gladly when pursuing every possible vote. Many, like Paudge

Brennan in the 1979 European elections, have felt a lash of Blaney's tongue after orders were not carried out to specification.

A story is told by Blaney supporters of an old man who attacked a Blaney poster outside a polling station in Sligo on the morning of polling day. 'Daylight robbers,' he repeatedly shouted, obviously believing the rumour which was circulating that a £45,000 bank robbery the previous day was organised to procure additional money for Blaney's election fund. Despite such rumours, the victory was overwhelming. He received 81,522 votes, surpassing the quota by some 5,000 votes as he was elected on the first count. At the count centre in Galway, his supporters were euphoric when the result was announced. Along with Paudge Brennan, Blaney was carried shoulder high out of the hall as his supporters broke into a deafening cry of, 'We want Blaney, we want Blaney'. In his acceptance speech Blaney said, 'I don't see this win as something to crow about. I wasn't there just to knock someone else. Throughout the campaign I presented myself to the electorate as the best man to send to Europe'. He was astonished by the extent of his vote, which he put down to a miracle. In relation to Fianna Fáil he said with some pleasure that, 'This vote I got may show them that I was more right than they were'. He added that one of the factors behind his victory was that, 'It was the first time that committed people really got a chance to vote for a solidly republican position.'

Within hours one of his supporters had attached an illuminated sign onto the roof of his car which was parked outside a hotel in Salthill. 'Blaney's In Europe,' it beamed brightly. Inside, Blaneyites from all over the country were celebrating and singing triumphantly, 'He's got Fianna Fáil in his hands. He's got Fianna Fáil in his hands. He's got the whole world in his hands'. For Jack Lynch, Blaney's election as an MEP in Connaught-Ulster, not to mention the size of his vote, was embarrassing. Many Fianna Fáil supporters had deserted the party and cast their vote for Blaney in a protest at Lynch's leadership. Overall, the European election results for Fianna Fáil were disappointing and they were one of the factors which led to the change in leadership some months later.

Throughout the 1979 European campaign Blaney had said that, if elected, he might consider joining one of the Euro-Parliament's political groupings – even the Gaullists, the group to which Fianna Fáil was at that time allied. There is little power for a solitary MEP in Brussels and Strasburg. Rather than aligning himself, however, with one of the existing groupings, Blaney rounded up a disparate number of fellow solitary MEPs ranging from left-wing Italian members to Flemish nationalists. Through a series of amendments to the rules of the Parliament and an all-night session, this motley crew got approval within the Parliament as a formal 'technical' grouping which is now known as the 'Rainbow Group'. This achievement won for its members the trappings reserved for already recognised groups. A former vice-chairperson of the Rainbow Group, Blaney is currently Treasurer of the Group.

In Europe, the Donegal man honoured his electoral promises as he assumed the mantle of spokesperson for one of the most remote and poorest regions within the European Community, while also raising questions relating to Northern Ireland whenever the opportunity presented itself. He involved himself as a member of the Parliament's Budgetary Control Committee and the Agriculture, Fisheries and Rural Development Committee. He listed his particular policy interests for a Parliament biography profile as 'agriculture, fisheries, education, environment and human rights'.

Blaney was an advocate at this stage, long before cohesion became fashionable as a concept in the Community, of increased regional and structural funding for the poorer regions in the European Community. In parliamentary debates he argued that there must be 'greater regional funds, and in order that they are spent to the greatest advantage, we must coordinate the common agricultural policy, where it affects the disadvantaged areas, with the Regional Fund itself, with the Social Fund and with our development funds'. He also used his membership of the Agriculture, Fisheries and Rural Development Committee to promote the interests of peripheral and less-developed regions. His Euro-constituency, Connaught-Ulster, was then, and remains today, one of the poorest regions in the European Community. Speaking in the Parliament in 1980 Blaney said, 'I come from a Connaught-Ulster constituency which is really the west and the north-west of Ireland. It is regarded as the poorest region in the present Community. We have, naturally, all the problems that have been experienced in all the other disadvantaged areas of the Community and, despite the efforts that may have been made, these disadvantages seem to increase, relatively speaking, over the years.' The north west of Ireland, Blaney says, 'has no scheduled air service, no railways and no access to sea transport, and our roads are in poor condition. That is the most peripheral part of the most peripheral country in the EC'.

The consequences of economic and social deprivation, contributed to by peripherality, was nothing new to Blaney, who since his youth had witnessed the impact of such factors in his home county of Donegal. In a 1991 *Irish Times* interview, Neil Blaney spoke about the uniqueness of his native county. 'We are an island within the island of Ireland. I do not think there is anyone in Donegal that will not assert, in stronger language maybe than I would use, that we do not belong at all in the twenty-six counties. We have the Border on one side and the Atlantic on the other. There is only three miles of land bordering the twenty-six.'

This 'island within the island' location contributes, Blaney feels, to depriving Donegal in a unique way. 'We are not given any special treatment because of our isolation and get little recompense from our own Government. For the first forty or fifty years of partition, our isolation was particularly dramatic. Derry should have been Donegal's hinterland. Now we are looking after ourselves to the best of our ability.' The closeness of its position to Northern Ireland has often created a feeling of dissatisfaction in Donegal. The people in

Donegal clearly see the superior standard of public services funded by the UK Exchequer available to those across the Border. It raises local expectations and their demands on local public representatives. In recent years, however, Donegal has done relatively better than in preceding times and the inflow of European Community funds has been a major factor in this progress.

Throughout his political career, Neil Blaney has put great trust in public sector investment in the construction industry as a means of rejuvenating the economy in times of economic stagnation. 'It has been shown over the years that when the construction industry is on its knees, so also is the economy.' When he struck the deal to support Charlie Haughey's nomination for Taoiseach in February 1982, one of the commitments Blaney sought was State support for the construction sector to spur the economy out of the economic depression which it was experiencing at that time. The real value from EC Structural Funds, Blaney believes, would be seen if it was spent in areas like public housing, rather than on training schemes. He said in the Dáil as recently as December 1992 that, 'Tackling the housing problem in a positive way would make a real dent in the unemployment figures and would give new impetus to the whole economy'. The housing crisis he feels is today as bad as at any time since 1948, when he was first elected to Dáil Eireann, and he argues that, 'Far from it costing the Government and the public Exchequer in the real sense, a massive building and construction programme would make money for the Government, the economy and the country'.

In the European Parliament Blaney had hoped to have some dialogue with the Northern Ireland MEPs like Ian Paisley, believing that away from the direct spotlight of Ireland contact could be made without any inhibitions. During the 1979 campaign he had said that he hoped to be closely identified with the MEPs from the North. 'Following a frosty start on their part, I have got to know them slightly better than I did,' Blaney later said. Relationships have, however, been difficult to build, with much of the mutual distrust transferring itself from Ireland to Europe. Blaney, himself, has not helped this process. On one occasion when addressing the Parliament he spoke of the Community's 'reluctance to face the unpalatable fact that one member of the Community is in fact occupying the territory of another and thereby denying the basic human right of self-determination.' Blaney lobbied for several months in the early 1980s until he got a parliamentary debate on the use of plastic bullets by the security forces in Northern Ireland. 'It is a total ban we want – not for Ireland, but for all the Community because these plastic bullets are lethal and they are being used indiscriminately,' Blaney said in his contribution to the debate. This debate in 1982 was one of the many occasions when Blaney and Ian Paisley clashed on the floor of the Parliament over issues relating to Northern Ireland. Nevertheless, Blaney still believes that co-operation on issues of mutual interest between MEPs from both sides of the Border is vital – 'West of the Bann and west of the Shannon are similar territory with similar problems'.

His membership of the Parliament enhanced his reputation and won respect from many of his fellow members. Europe broadened his views and it has been said by some that it matured him as an individual and as a politician. Blaney's involvement in the Technical/Rainbow Group led to an embracement of many new causes such as the nuclear arms race, hunger in the Developing World and human rights' abuses internationally. In this period as an MEP, Blaney contributed to parliamentary debate on issues as diverse as the persecution of the Kurdish people in Turkey and the Irish rugby team's tour to South Africa in 1980 to which he was opposed. Certainly it would have been unlikely that the pre-1979 Neil Blaney would have objected to the visit of US President Ronald Regan to Ireland. The Neil Blaney with the added European dimension to his character most certainly did. In explaining why he would be boycotting Regan's address to the Oireachtas, Blaney said that he disagreed fundamentally with the US President's Central American policy and with his continuing escalation of the nuclear arms race. Given such profile and such stances it was all the more disappointing for Blaney when he lost his seat in 1984.

The defeat was a bitter blow. It was his first electoral defeat since his entry into politics in 1948. He attributes the defeat to his organisation who, after the success in 1979, did not believe that they would have to fight to hold the seat, especially given that he was 5,000 votes in excess of the quota on the first count in 1979. 'I knew for weeks and weeks that it wasn't going to happen. The reason was terribly evident. We swept the boards in '79 totally against all predictions and in 1984 nothing would make my supporters believe that we had anything to do other than to just mosie along up to election day and celebrate on the day of the count. Nothing could change their minds.'

He also feels that an unspoken pact between Fianna Fáil and Fine Gael not to have any great competition contributed to his defeat. 'It was a no-contest election, low keyed down to the bare turn-out of the hardliners in each party. Whereas if we had a real turn-out, I'd have retained the seat,' Blaney now says, as he recalls the difficulty he had in getting the candidates of the main parties to debate the issues on the same platform with him at public meetings throughout Connaught-Ulster.

Blaney was also faced with a strong united challenge from Fianna Fáil in 1984. The party had on its ticket Ray McSharry, who was using the 1984 European elections as a means of re-building his political career. The former Tánaiste and Minister for Agriculture and for Finance had been involved in controversy, following the revelations that he had taped a conversation with party colleague Martin O'Donoghue in 1982, during one of the heaves against Charles Haughey's leadership of Fianna Fáil. All the predictions were, however, that McSharry would take his running mate Seán Flanagan's seat and that Blaney would be safe. Flanagan, who had captained Mayo to GAA All-Ireland titles in 1950 and 1951, was a former Cabinet colleague of Blaney. Like Blaney he was defending the European Parliamentary seat he had won in 1979. Just prior to

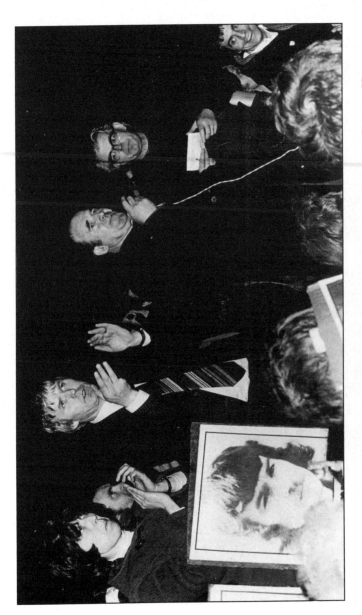

Dublin, 22 November 1980. National H-Block Committee march and rally outside Leinster House.

(Derek Speirs / Report)

Euro MPs hold press conference in Dublin, 20 April 1981, following their visit to Bobby Sands M.P. on hunger strike in the Maze prison. (Derek Speirs / Report)

Belfast, 4 August 1981. Neil Blaney attends the funeral of Kieran Doherty T.D. (Derek Speirs / Report)

Bundoran, 18 June 1984. Blaney in conversation with one of his supporters on the night he lost his Euro-seat in 1984. (Donegal Democrat)

The Independent Fianna Fail Republican Party

Mr. Brian Gallagher N.T.,
Neilands,
Drumboe,
Ballybofey,
Co. Donegal.

21st October, 1985.

Mr. Charles J. Haughey,
Abbeyville,
Kinsealy,
Co. Dublin.

Dear Mr. Haughey,

Over the years, and in particular during the past twelve months, there is evidence of a persistent and widespread demand that our two parties reconcile their differences in the interests of our Country.

Your recent statements on major policy matters and on the National issues in particular shows no significant differences from our party's point of view.

The support of our Organisation for you when in Government and at other crucial times has been consistent, even when to our detriment. The co-operation between our parties during the recent Local Elections campaign, and since, has resulted in our parties jointly taking control of all the elected bodies and their committees in counties Leitrim, Louth, Roscommon and Donegal.

We therefore request that you meet with a delegation from our party to discuss the amalgamation of our respective Organisations and have the matter resolved one way or the other.

If you accede to this request, we suggest that the meeting be held at the earliest possible date, and before the run-up to your next Ard Fheis commences.

SIGNED: *Daniel Mc Guinness*

Mr. D. McGuinness, Chairman

Brian G. Gallagher

Mr. B. Gallagher, Secretary.

*Letter from Daniel McGuinness and Brian Gallagher
of Independent Fianna Fáil to Charles Haughey.*

Donegal North East deputies, from left to right, Paddy Harte (Fine Gael), Neil Blaney Independent Fianna Fáil, Dr Jim McDaid (Fianna Fáil). (Jon Carlos / The Sunday Tribune)

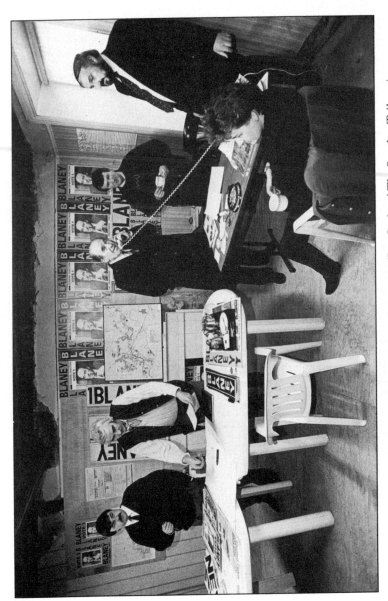

Election '92. Blaney in his Donegal headquarters. (Jon Carlos / The Sunday Tribune)

'Focusing'

Neil Blaney focuses in on his twelfth election campaign, pictured at his Independent Fianna Fáil headquarters over his family-run pub on Letterkenny Main Street. (*The Donegal Democrat*)

the 1984 elections, Flanagan announced proposals for a £500 million development package for the west of Ireland, although he studiously refused to answer questions on the proposal during the election campaign. It may have been greeted with scepticism nationally, but Blaney today sees what he calls 'the plan that never was', as contributing to his narrow defeat by Flanagan. The GAA was celebrating its centenary in 1984 and RTE was re-showing many famous matches throughout the year. Blaney is critical of the decision to show in full the two Mayo All-Ireland football wins with Flanagan as captain in the weeks prior to voting, a decision which he believes 'was not an accident whatsoever by whoever designed it'.

In the end, Blaney's defeat was down to McSharry's determination to take a seat, combined with his organisation's lack-lustre campaign, which was not helped by his own ill-health in the run-in to polling-day which cut down on his personal appearances. Blaney received just over 32,000 votes, well down on his handsome vote in 1979. The count in Bundoran was shrouded in drama, as Blaney's election agent sought a recount after the result of the first count was announced. Despite Blaney's ability to substantially claw back the near 8,000 first count margin between himself and Seán Flanagan with the help of transfers, in the end the sitting Fianna Fáil MEP beat him by some 1,500 votes. 'I was defeated by one vote in each polling station on average, in 1,500 polling stations. It was the most frustrating election I ever fought for the reason that I knew that we had the votes but not the type of campaign to get them out. Had my people fought the election on the day after the count, I'd have got in with twice the number I had – such was my organisation's disappointment.'

Down but certainly by no means out, Neil Blaney and his supporters 'waited in the long grass', as he says himself. His supporters were on their toes in 1989 when Blaney was successfully returned to the European Parliament. He added some 20,000 first preference votes to the 32,000 he had received in 1984 and although the outcome was still well off his 1979 vote, it was enough to see him comfortably elected.

In many ways, Blaney's victory in 1989 was a greater political achievement than the success of ten years previously when he was first elected to the European Parliament with over 80,000 first preference votes. In 1979 the Fianna Fáil ticket was weak. Seán Flanagan, who had lost his Dáil seat in the 1977 general election, was the strongest of the three Fianna Fáil candidates and many party supporters backed Blaney out of resentment with the leadership of Jack Lynch. In 1989, Blaney faced a strong Fianna Fáil challenge from sitting MEP Mark Killilea and Seán Doherty, a former Cabinet Minister. In addition, he was forced to fight the European election alongside a general election. 'The double in 1989 more than made up for the defeat in '84,' he says as he refers to the calling of a general election on the same day as the European Parliamentary elections in June 1989. With a smile on his face he comments, 'They celebrated when I was beaten in '84, but they probably wept when I retrieved the seat in '89, against all the odds. I am the only member of the 518 member European Parliament who was in it, beaten and came back.'

Back in Europe, Neil Blaney once again became a member of the Agriculture, Fisheries and Rural Development Committee. He is also a substitute member of the Budgetary Control Committee and the Committee on Rules of Procedure, Verification of Credentials and Immunities. A colleague in the European Parliament, Munster MEP T.J. Maher, says that 'Blaney never hesitates to state his views and he is quite forceful. Northern Ireland, Agriculture and Fisheries are his three main policy areas'. Blaney has been criticised for holding seats in both the Dáil and the European Parliament, the so-called 'dual mandate'. Yet, he appears to have successfully managed both jobs which, in reality, are no more demanding than the position of Government Minister who also must fulfil the duties of a TD. Nevertheless, since 1989 Blaney's contributions have been more frequent in Europe than in Dáil Eireann – he spoke on only nine occasions in the last Dáil and his record has been no better in the present Dáil. Brian Lenihan, however, defends his old Cabinet colleague's speaking record. 'He speaks when he has to speak in key debates. We have too much bloody quantity and nonsense here in this House – quality is what we want and anytime Blaney speaks he is listened to. The quality of his speeches is very good.'

Neil Blaney, himself, puts his Dáil speaking record down to the ease of getting speaking time in the European Parliament when compared to Dáil Eireann. He has constantly bemoaned the attitude adopted towards Independent deputies by the main political parties in relation to procedures such as the allocation of speaking time. Those TDs who are not members of a registered political party of at least seven members are debarred from certain privileges enjoyed by the members of mainstream parties like Fine Gael, Labour and Fianna Fáil. Blaney used the nomination debate for the present Government in the Dáil to raise this situation. 'We have been elected and we have the right to speak. We represent an electorate and we are entitled to be heard in this forum, if it is to continue to be regarded as a democratic institution.' In the present Dáil the Independent TDs, including Blaney and the four Democratic Left deputies, have come together to form a 'Technical Group' which allows them to benefit from group privileges. Blaney has also suggested that the Dáil committee system be designed along the lines of that which exists in the European Parliament, where each of the 518 members is a full member of at least one committee and a substitute member of at least one other committee.

Blaney has repeatedly criticised the Brussels' red tape and regrets that in many instances 'the layers of bureaucracy make the Parliament a facade'. He says that he is pro-European, but apprehensive about the pace of integration since the passing of the *Single European Act 1987*. It was because of such apprehensions that he opposed both the SEA and the more recent Maastricht Treaty on European Union. A reliable source says that Blaney 'felt that there was not nearly enough consultation at home in Ireland and that the implications of the Treaty were poorly thought out. Obviously, he also had problems with the abortion protocol'. In 1993 he told *The Sunday Business Post* that, 'Delors is the wrong man in the wrong place at the right time. To bring together, so quickly, nations which were not so long ago at war with each other is just not on'.

— 8 —
The Republican Motivation

On 1 March 1981 Bobby Sands, a republican prisoner at the Maze/Long Kesh prison outside Belfast, went on hunger strike. In the succeeding months nine other prisoners were to follow Sands in fasting to their deaths, in an attempt to convince the British Government to meet their demands. The prisoners in the Maze were seeking five 'rights' which had been a matter of contention for several years: the right to wear their own clothes; to refrain from prison work; to organise recreational facilities; to have one letter, parcel and visit a week; and to have lost remission time restored.

The use of the hunger strike was a continuation of the 'blanket' and 'dirty' protests, when prisoners convicted of what would, in other circumstances, have been described as politically motivated crimes refused to wear prison clothing. Such clothing was seen as the symbol of an ordinary prisoner and in protest the prisoners covered the walls, floors and ceilings of their cells with their excrement. As this 'dirty' protest failed to bring any improvement in their situation the prisoners turned to the hunger strike.

Neil Blaney was one of the first politicians in the Republic to highlight the cause of the men in Long Kesh and to see the potential bloody implications of the deaths of Sands and his fellow hunger strikers. Speaking at the time he said – ' We have a most frightening situation in the H-Blocks at the moment, arising from the occupation and oppression over the centuries'. As always, Blaney was consistent in his understanding of the issue, seeing the kernel of the problem as rooted in the British presence in the Six Counties.

In Ireland, the hunger strike was increasingly used for political purposes after the Easter Rising of 1916. In late 1917 Thomas Ashe, a participant in the Rising and former President of the Irish

Republican Brotherhood, went on hunger strike after refusing to work or wear prison clothes. He died after he was force-fed in an attempt to end his hunger strike in Mountjoy Prison. Three years later, in October 1920, Terence MacSwiney, who had been elected Lord Mayor of Cork in March of the same year, died in Brixton prison, after a seventy-three day hunger strike that gained worldwide attention and earned MacSwiney an Apostolic Blessing and Plenary Indulgence from Pope Benedict XV.

Following in the tradition of Ashe and MacSwiney, several republican prisoners over the period since independence have fasted to their deaths, primarily for the right to be classified as 'political prisoners'. Among these was Frank Stagg, a brother of Labour Party TD and Government Minister Emmet Stagg, who died on hunger strike in an English jail in 1976. Stagg was laid to rest following a farcical affair over his body, during which the coffin was literally hijacked at Shannon airport by the Special Branch and interred under six feet of concrete at a plot which was not that chosen by Stagg prior to his death. Speaking in the Dáil at the time, Neil Blaney challenged the then Minister for Justice, Fine Gael's Paddy Cooney, saying that the 'whole performance surrounding the funeral of the late Frank Stagg, was totally and absolutely unnecessary'. Some months later, after the Gardai had grown tired of standing guard outside the cemetery and departed, the IRA tunnelled under the concrete and removed the coffin to the republican plot nearby. The 1981 hunger strike in the Long Kesh followed in this long line of passive resistance.

Bobby Sands was the sole nationalist candidate in the Fermanagh-Tyrone by-election caused by the death of the incumbent nationalist MP, Frank Maguire. It would have been difficult for another member of the nationalist community to stand against Sands, who had the moral force of the hunger strike on his side. The Northern Ireland Office had refused to allow Sands any freedom to campaign, such as the right to be interviewed on television. From his prison cell, where he was refusing food, Sands had his election campaign run by the likes of Owen Carron, Gerry Adams and former MP Bernadette McAliskey. The campaign was backed on the ground by republicans from all parts of Ireland who descended on the constituency in their cars, flying tricolours and blaring republican songs from loudspeakers. Blaney too played his part. While campaigning in Fermanagh prior to polling day, he declared that votes for Sands would 'highlight to the world the barbarous treatment meted out in the H-Block and Armagh'. The Official Unionist candidate, Harry West, denounced Blaney's involvement in the campaign and described Blaney as an 'IRA fellow-traveller'. It was criticism the Donegal man took lightly, and even as the election of Sands to Westminster, with over 30,000 votes, totally transformed the status of the hunger strike, Blaney continued in his efforts to find a solution to the hunger strike.

On the 51st day of Sands' fast he was visited by three members of Dáil Éireann – Síle de Valera, Dr John O'Connell and Neil Blaney. In explaining the reason behind the visit Blaney says – 'He invited us to meet him, as three people whom he knew, by repute, to be concerned about his position and about others in similar circumstances'. The three, who were also members of the European Parliament, met at the Fairways Hotel in Dundalk in the early hours of a Monday morning because the RUC, for security reasons, wanted them across the Border by 7.30 a.m. Owen Carron and Danny Morrison of Sinn Féin met them at the hotel and took them by car across the Border where an RUC vehicle was waiting to take them the thirty miles or so to Long Kesh.

Despite their status as TDs and MEPs, all three were searched on entering the prison complex. They were brought to the prison hospital and a warden made Sands aware of their arrival with – 'You've got visitors, members of the European Parliament'. Sands, who had been given the Last Rites the previous Saturday, was at this stage sleeping on a sheep-skin rug, on a water-bed, in an attempt to protect his skin. He was barely audible and they had to lean over him to hear. Sands spoke to them for almost forty minutes about his recent election, the background to the hunger strikes and how the five demands could be met by Britain without any loss of face. O'Connell asked him to give up the fast but Sands refused, merely replying to him, 'I knew you would say that'. Neither Blaney nor de Valera agreed with O'Connell's actions. Blaney's attitude to the request was simple – 'I did not think that this kind of torture should be added to his condition'. Recalling the visit to Long Kesh Blaney says, 'My abiding impression is of a man who had made his decision – who with great sadness had made it because of his belief that what he was doing may bring about a change in the situation that had driven him to the extremity that he was then in'.

The parting was highly emotional with Síle de Valera in tears. In his book, *Ten Men Dead*, journalist David Beresford writes of the farewells between Sands and his visitors – 'Blaney, big and tough by reputation, bent over to say goodbye, and caressed Sands' face with the back of his hand in a gesture of intense gentleness'. Dr John O'Connell recalls – 'Neil Blaney I had always seen as a strong man. He was very gentle on that occasion. You see a man in a different light when you see him supporting someone's republicanism, holding his hand gently, full of concern for Sands . . . Síle and Neil both told him he was a hero'.

They were taken out of Long Kesh through a side gate because there was a Loyalist demonstration against their visit taking place at the front gate. They had planned to go to Belfast to hold a press conference – but the RUC insisted that they had to return south of the Border. At an alternative press conference in Dublin, they appealed to Mrs Thatcher to meet them to discuss the prison dispute. Mrs Thatcher, who was on a visit to Saudi Arabia, responded negatively – 'It is not my habit to meet MPs from a foreign country about a citizen of the United Kingdom, resident in the United Kingdom'. Blaney later noted that the visit, 'failed to open up new avenues for a resolution of the H-Block crisis'. Despite this disappointment Blaney continued in his efforts to find a resolution to the hunger strike, which by this time saw three other prisoners join Sands on the fast.

Blaney travelled to Westminster in late April 1981 to make what he describes as an 'eleventh hour appeal' to the British Government to make concessions on the H-Block hunger strikers' demands to end the strike. A protest about his presence at Westminster came from the Derry Official Unionist MP, Mr William Ross, who asked the then Prime Minister whether she was aware 'that the IRA gun-runner is to address a meeting later in the afternoon'. Mrs Thatcher, who had resisted all attempts to get her Government to interfere in the hunger strike, replied curtly – 'the use of any rooms in the House is not a matter for me but for the authorities of the House'. At a bizarre hour-long press conference in a House of Commons committee room, questions were asked of Blaney about his political background and beliefs. The Arms Crisis was never far away and pressed by journalists about whether he had ever 'run guns' Blaney replied – 'I have not, if you particularly want to know'.

On Tuesday 5 May 1981 Bobby Sands died. Blaney continued to use his position and status to gain support for the hunger strikers' campaign. Along with Síle de Valera, he sought the inclusion of a motion on the issue on the official agenda of the European Parliament and requested that a letter of sympathy be sent to Sands' family. Further efforts by Blaney to raise the issue in Dáil Éireann were equally unsuccessful. On one occasion when he was ruled out of order by the then Ceann Comhairle, Padraig Faulkner, he stormed out of the Dáil Chamber shouting in disgust, 'You will go down in history' and other words which were inaudible and not recorded.

Neil Blaney outlined the context within which his political make-up had been formed and the beliefs that motivate him, in his address to the Dáil following his dismissal as Minister for Agriculture and Fisheries in May 1970. It explains to a great extent why Blaney holds the views that he does, why he involved himself to the extent that he did in the hunger strikers' campaign and why, in recent years, he opposed both extradition and the Anglo-Irish Agreement.

'I could not but be Fianna Fáil and republican unless I was to renege the heritage of my parents before me. I was born while my late father was under sentence of death. He was again on the run. A few years later, as a child, I was kicked out of the cot I lay in by one of the forces of the then alleged nation . . .We come later then to 1926 and even at four years of age, even at that young age, I remember, believe it or not, the raids of the Irregulars and the Special Branch of that day. I remember my mother and I, as a child, and others of my family being terrified by these fellows who were as often drunk as they were sober when they came on these raids, perhaps because, having sold out their republican principles, they had to drown their shame in liquor. I remember it. I shall never forget it.

'And let nobody in this House or outside ever try to tell me what should be my outlook in so far as the unification of this country is concerned because this is the way I was brought into being. This is the way I was reared. That is the way my thought has been developed. My guidance comes from that source. At this particular time I derive great strength from my past, from my breeding, from my father and mother, both of whom have gone to their reward. These things I cannot forget. These things I do not want to trot out, but these things must be said in order that people fully understand where I stand and how I come to stand there and how I came to be in Fianna Fáil right over the years, working as I did, for I was a child in Fianna Fáil, being kicked by a Blueshirt black and blue on my way from school because I displayed on the lapel of my coat, or jacket, or jersey or whatever it was, the tricolour that these people would never stand up and give honour to. Well I remember it. I shall never forget it. I try to forgive but never to forget. Let us keep things in mind. I shall keep them in mind, but let us also keep in mind that, as those years went on, I became part of Fianna Fáil. I could not be otherwise because it was founded with one primary aim of trying to undo the partition of this land of ours, which has given so much trouble, so much pain and is continuing to do just that, and will continue to do it in lesser or greater measure so long as unity and unification have not been brought about. I apologise to no one for my views and the views I hold in regard to the reunification of Ireland.'

The achievement of a united Ireland is Neil Blaney's ultimate ambition. It is an aim shared by political colleagues right across the political spectrum in Ireland. Neil Blaney, however, sees the ending of partition and the withdrawal of British troops from Northern Ireland as the twin tasks necessary to achieve such an ambition. Irish society has moved in such a way over the last twenty years that people like Neil Blaney, who see the Northern situation in terms of partition and British withdrawal, are increasingly perceived as marginal and irrelevant. Maurice Dockrell, a Fine Gael deputy until the late 1970s, remarked of Neil Blaney that, 'He forces his mind into the past and lashes himself with pity'. The opinion of many people would probably be expressed by Des O'Malley when he argues that, 'It's sad to see people burying themselves in the illusions of the past. They seem to think that the problems which Ireland has in the 1990s are the same that we had in the 1920s and that's just nonsense'. Even Brian Lenihan, who says that he respects and shares Blaney's desire to see a united Ireland, perceives the Blaney line on the North as argued in Cabinet in 1969-70 as most definitely outdated for the Ireland of the 1990s. 'While I could understand his attitude at that time, the important thing in politics is change. We're twenty-five years further on now . . . you must look for new formulae to deal with the problem. You're not going to handle this situation unless there is new thinking . . . you must move the situation forward.'

To Neil Blaney the events of the 1920s and before are, however, central to defining the Irish nation. Neil Blaney's republicanism is certainly rooted in history but he is no slave to history – his belief does have contemporary meaning which comes from living in such close proximity to the Six Counties. To him the Border is an artificial entity which is the root of the Northern problem and to tackle the problem one must go to its root. In his often mentioned, but little read, Letterkenny speech of November 1969, Blaney explicitly outlines why he considers the partitioning of the island offensive.

'The majority in the Six Counties has no moral right to decide on partition, for the very logical reason that the Six Counties was, and still is, an artificial creation set up against the majority wishes of the Irish people, and drawn up on the sole basis of giving the Unionists as much territory as they could maintain, and that only by gerrymander and discrimination. Carson has told us, for instance, why he did not take in the whole nine counties of Ulster in his conception of an Orange State. The reason that there were at that time some 275,000 Catholics living alongside 72,000 Protestants in the counties of Donegal, Cavan and Monaghan. These figures would have upset the Unionist majority in the other six Ulster counties . . . To say that the majority within the Six Counties should have the right to decide on partition is to accept that partition was in the first justified. Ireland was partitioned against the wishes of her people, and it is the majority of the people of all Ireland who alone have the right to decide this question. This is the primary civil right of all.'

Contrary to the belief of many, Neil Blaney's united Ireland would be all encompassing, taking in all traditions. 'I have been reared in a mixed community. I know the people of all religions. I have been reared among them, gone to school with them, danced and played with them . . . I have a feeling for all our people, not for any particular section.' He said in an interview some years ago that, 'My dear, final wish will always be that if and when we get to the stage of Britain going, we then will be in a position to ceremoniously, with no disrespect to either, drop a symbolic crown and a copy of the Irish Constitution dead centre in the middle of the Irish sea', adding that then all interested parties could sit down and write a new constitution for the new political framework that would exist. While Blaney has been unequivocal in outlining his solutions to the Northern Troubles he has been less articulate in suggesting what comes should British troops withdraw from Northern Ireland and partition end. He has constantly challenged the British and Irish Governments to put together a plan for the time when a united Ireland arrives, but he has himself been slow to clearly outline his vision for such a thirty-two county Ireland.

One observer has remarked that while Blaney's views 'are passionately held, they do today come across as jaded and clichéd mainly because he has repeatedly stated them in the same way and in the same style'. It is certainly true that arousing the interest of the general Irish public in events in Northern Ireland is at the best of times difficult. Unfortunately, for politicians like Neil Blaney, to whom the question of Northern Ireland is so central to their political motivation, these issues are simply not politically relevant to the general public.

The reaction to the bombings in Warrington in early 1993 best illustrates the attitude of probably the majority of the population of the Irish Republic to the events in Northern Ireland. That it took IRA atrocities in England to awaken a public feeling of anger to what is almost daily carnage on their own island speaks volumes of the amnesia concerning the Troubles which exists on this island. Mark Brennock, former Northern Ireland correspondent for *The Irish Times* recalls the frustration of trying to interest people in the conflict. 'After six months in the job in Belfast, I was on a visit to Dublin. A TD approached me in Doheny and Nesbitt's pub and asked where I had been, and if I had left *The Irish Times*. He hadn't seen anything written by me in the newspaper for months, he said. He was surprised to hear that I was working in Belfast and that I was writing copious amounts for the paper. The problem was, I told him, that many of the articles had the words North, Brooke or killing in the headline, and he was probably one of those who didn't read such articles. He agreed.'

It is not so easy for the people of Donegal to walk away from the violence. 'We live beside it and, in many ways, know the people involved and it is happening to us even though it is not happening in Donegal. We are very conscious of it and we suffer dreadfully in commercial and tourism terms,' Blaney says. 'You get used to the violence but you do not accept it.'

Blaney sees the Provisional IRA as a symptom rather than a cause of the Troubles in Northern Ireland and his refusal to publicly condemn their actions has certainly lessened his potential impact when he addresses the question of Northern Ireland. While he acknowledges that the IRA campaign is unlikely ever to be in a position to bring about a solution in the North, he says that he neither supports nor condemns the organisation. He told one interviewer that his 'aims, as stated before 1970, are the same as those that Sinn Féin and the IRA would now proclaim, but I was stating those aims long before there was a Provisional IRA'. Blaney, who had absolutely no part in the establishment of the Provisionals, explains his refusal to condemn the actions of the IRA in terms of the Republic's lack of support for the nationalist community in the North. 'Since we opted out . . . and thereby denied our responsibility for the concerns, and the protection of, our citizens North as well as South, we have no real right to criticise how, on being left to their own devices, they do things to look after themselves.'

He sees no reason for optimism about the current talks initiative between the parties in the North and the Irish and British Governments. 'The situation is not going to change. There isn't a hope that it will be any different in 1999 than it was in 1969 unless there is a complete new approach by Britain. The only untried solution is their getting out. Unless that happens then I'll die as it is and the next generation will die and it will be no different.' He is critical of the Irish Government and feels that 'Dublin is nearly afraid of unity'. In the period since the current 'Troubles' began Blaney feels that views have become more strongly held. 'There are now "hardened soldiers" on both sides of the divide. A large proportion are now hardened soldiers of both points of view, supported by the vast majority of the communities of both sides. Paramilitaries cannot exist without massive support of their communities. It is this support which sustains these soldiers.'

When Neil Blaney speaks about Northern Ireland and the IRA's campaign of violence he makes many in the Republic uncomfortable. This is partly because his thinking on the subject exposes the contradictions that riddle the poorly thought out words of many in the Irish Republic who would call themselves Republicans. 'I feel a crawling sensation when I hear people talking about the great men of the IRA of 1916-22 and after, and then a total denigration of the people who are giving their lives today – even if they may be misdirected, even if they may be misled. Nobody can say that they are not men of conviction'.

It is difficult to reconcile these sentiments with the fact that, as one Fine Gael source puts it, 'Blaney was a member of Fianna Fáil Governments which jailed Republicans without trial in the mid-'50s and which introduced Special Military Courts so as to hand out excessive sentences to the IRA in the early 1960s'. When questioned by one journalist in the early 1980s about these 'republican struggles', Blaney fudged the issue by claiming that, 'In so far as I was a member of the Government and the Dáil, I recognised the sovereignty of that Dáil and that Government. We were dealing with people who were a danger to that sovereignty. The difference between then and now is the difference between chalk and cheese'.

Nevertheless, it has to be said that his lack of directness in relation to his opinions on the activities of the Provisional IRA has left Blaney's views open to misinterpretation and has resulted in his opinions being treated with a degree of suspicion. Of all his beliefs and convictions with regard to Northern Ireland those which Blaney articulates regarding the activities of the IRA are those which do him least favour. 'Neil Blaney is a nationalist who seems to have very little convention about using violence to achieve nationalist ends,' according to Dick Walsh of *The Irish Times*. 'People can accept the conviction regarding partition and the presence of the British army, but they expect condemnation of the IRA, no matter what the position of the local nationalist community in Northern Ireland,' says one colleague.

Neil Blaney is on record in his support for the retention of the constitutional claims over the Six Counties which articles 2 and 3 of Bunreacht na hÉireann assert. 'Articles 2 and 3 cannot and must not be put on the table to pander to hard line Unionists who are giving nothing whatsoever in return,' Blaney argues, while adding that, 'Article 75 of the *Ireland Act* must be on the table alongside those two Articles. I say this with the greatest conviction as a Northerner, an Ulsterman, as a neighbour of these people and as a deputy who is elected by many of their brethren on my side of the Border. It is nonsense to say that Articles 2 and 3 must be abandoned. This is an absolute historical claim which cannot be abandoned while Britain claims and occupies part of our country.'

The Anglo-Irish Agreement Blaney has described as ' a nonsense and a waste of time'. He has opposed the agreement since it was signed as a step away from the real issue of British withdrawal. 'The one good thing that emerged from it is that it has given some members who would otherwise never have gone to Belfast an opportunity to meet with some of the people there and see the conditions there. However, when members of the Government visit the North they are given guided tours and do not know what is going on.' The embracing of the accord by Charlie Haughey and Fianna Fáil when they went back into Government in 1987, after their outright rejection while in Opposition, ended any desire on Blaney's behalf to return to the party.

He has hard-hitting words for Fianna Fáil's attitude to Northern Ireland. 'Jack Lynch's Fianna Fáil and Charlie Haughey's Fianna Fáil have been a national disaster, a national tragedy paralleled only by the actual tragedy on the ground up North. Fianna Fáil is partly responsible. If we had de Valera or even Lemass during 1969 leading Fianna Fáil I think that the Troubles would have been finished long ago. We would be an Ireland, not necessarily united as a political unit, but we would have been an independent island without outside occupation, well on our way to having a united Ireland and a peaceful Ireland.'

He also believes that had he himself been elected leader of Fianna Fáil in 1966 the British Government would no longer be politically or militarily involved in the North of Ireland. The loss of the republican ethos in Fianna Fáil means to Neil Blaney that the party is no longer the party of his father's time, or the Fianna Fáil party for which he was first elected in 1948. 'God knows I can't tell you what it is. They don't know. I don't know. I don't think anybody else knows, but it's not Fianna Fáil.'

The Fianna Fáil party, Blaney feels, is today no different from any other political party, while he regrets that it has become dominated by 'politicians of opportunity'. Nevertheless, Neil Blaney is still holding out on a judgement on the leadership of Albert Reynolds. He voted for Reynolds' nomination for Taoiseach after the 1992 general election. He said in the Dáil at the time, 'He is the one Taoiseach I have known in my long time in this House who got no honeymoon after his election . . . Deputy Reynolds has more to give than we have yet seen from him'.

Albert Reynolds attended the Arms Trial proceedings in 1970. It was seven years before he was to enter Dáil Éireann and over another decade before he was elected Taoiseach. Over this entire period Neil Blaney has remained on the Independent benches in Dáil Éireann yet, despite this position, he has far from become 'peripheral'. His election to the European Parliament has ensured that his views, and the views of his supporters have not become 'yesterday's views'. Those who have watched Blaney's political organisation in Donegal have commented that while the bulk of his supporters are of his own age group there are a few younger supporters prepared to continue the Blaney tradition. There is a kind of silent belief that one day the rest of the island will have to face up to the issues such as partition, empowering local communities and the destruction of agriculture, which Neil Blaney has been preaching about for over the last two decades. With or without Neil Blaney as their figure-head, his younger supporters are intent that when that day comes they will be prepared to continue the Blaney legacy. Whether they do so within an Independent organisation or within the Fianna Fáil party fold itself remains to be seen.

Neil Blaney, however, has not faded away as the script written for him by the Fianna Fáil Party in 1972 foresaw. Indeed, despite his position as an Independent deputy, Neil Blaney has been centrally involved in some of the most dramatic events in recent Irish political life. After the Fine Gael-Labour Coalition Government fell in January 1982, Blaney found himself in a meeting with Charles Haughey who was of the opinion that he could lead a minority Fianna Fáil administration, without the need for a general election. Senior Fianna Fáil figures believed that President Paddy Hillery could use his constitutional prerogative to refuse Garrett FitzGerald a dissolution of the Dáil and call on Haughey to put together an alternative Government. The events of January 1982 were to assume a vital significance during the 1990 Presidential election when Brian Lenihan, the Fianna Fáil candidate, found his campaign, which was on course for victory, in turmoil over the issue of whether or not phone calls were made to the President in an attempt to get him to ask Charles Haughey to form a Government. In early 1990 in a taped interview with Jim Duffy, a UCD student who was researching the Presidency for a postgraduate thesis, Lenihan admitted that he had phoned the Áras on the night that the FitzGerald Government fell in 1982. The fact that phone calls were made to Hillery was well known, but what was new was Lenihan's acknowledgement that he had actually made these to the President.

Speaking on RTE during the Presidential election in 1990, Lenihan denied adamantly that he had telephoned Áras an Uachtaráin. In possession of taped evidence to the contrary Duffy made his supposedly confidential interview with Lenihan available to *The Irish Times*. There are good reasons for believing that senior Fine Gael figures were aware of the existence of the tape for some time. When the taped interview was made public, the Lenihan campaign was blown totally off track.

Neil Blaney had been involved in the attempt in 1982 to get Hillery to call on Charlie Haughey to become Taoiseach, by virtue of the position he held as an Independent TD whose support was necessary for such a plan to come off. 'We tried very hard that night, but the President wouldn't play ball! The bollocks! But yes, I did see it as an opportunity for a President to operate his prerogative not to dissolve the Dáil, by necessity, at the request of a beaten Taoiseach. I thought it was a damn good opportunity for Paddy Hillery to, in one act, be President. But the boy in the Park wouldn't function.' This admission in an interview with *Hot Press* magazine early in 1990 was to bring a touch of humour, which would have been lost on many on that eventful night when Charlie Haughey dismissed Brian Lenihan as Minister for Defence and Tánaiste prior to polling day in the 1990 Presidential election. Blaney rose to speak in the debate on Lenihan's dismissal, but before addressing that issue he felt obliged to refer to his *Hot Press* interview. 'I want to unreservedly withdraw what I said in that interview. I am sorry that such unparliamentary language should have been used by me, or anybody else, so far as our President is concerned.' The then President, Paddy Hillery, who had served in Cabinet with Blaney and would have vehemently opposed Blaney's views on Northern Ireland, would have been grateful!

One seasoned observer of the political scene has remarked that, 'Blaney's republicanism is much more complex than a one-dimensional view on Northern Ireland. His organisation has well thought out views, for example, empowering local communities'. Neil Blaney has used his membership of the European Community to articulate his views on these issues which are as central to his political make-up as the question of partition, but which, more often than not, receive little public attention. The fact that he is perceived as a one-dimensional politician is a source of personal annoyance which was very clearly expressed in an interview with *The Sunday Business Post.* 'With some exceptions, anytime I've been interviewed, it's been on the North and on the IRA. I'm totally ignored as a former chairman of Donegal County Council, a Minister for Local Government, of Fisheries, Agriculture, and P and T, or Communications as they call it now. No programme has ever sought me to talk about any of those Departments. You see them seeking people who don't know their arses from their elbows. I resent this very much because I'm not one-dimensional. Never was.'

While partition does remain the pivotal motivating force in Neil Blaney's life, he has well thought out and developed opinions on issues that he believes are central to Ireland's future. He has lived through the decimation of rural, agricultural life over the last number of years, with the CAP and GATT reform processes bearing ill-winds. As a former Minister for Agriculture Blaney is well aware of the concerns and needs of the farming community. It is his belief that, 'Farming can be written off in ten years time. There will not be another generation of farmers in Ireland. There will be ranchers but not family farms as we know them'. With some regret he says that Ireland is 'going down the tube as a small farming community and that it is the loss of all'. During his first term as an MEP Blaney was calling on the Community to structure the CAP to preserve the social fabric of agriculture by providing assistance for small farmers to remain on the land.

Blaney still places great faith in the ability of the construction sector to lift the economy out of recession. He repeatedly calls for state investment in this sector. A housing programme is one of the elements he feels would kick-start the economy. It is interesting to observe that still, after all these years, in his speeches on major topics he almost always brings Donegal examples into his addresses. When calling for an investment boost for the construction industry he will point to the need for new schools in Milford and when he makes a case for how EC Structural Funds should be allocated he will mention the lack of a regional airport in the north-west, and then will put forward Letterkenny as a possible location. When one former associate says that for Blaney Donegal is the centre of Ireland, if not the universe, he is totally accurate. Neil Blaney, while a national and a European politician, is, above all else, a local politician who has never failed to remember the county he represents.

The world in which Neil Blaney currently practises politics is totally removed from that which prevailed in 1948 when he was first elected to Dáil Éireann. Dick Walsh does not believe that 'there is a sufficient degree of openness to take in and embrace all the changes' which have come, particularly over the last two decades, although Walsh does admit that Blaney 'has become a good deal more open since he went to Europe'. For Neil Blaney the twin issues of generating economic growth and ending partition still dominate over all other issues. His view of the so-called 'liberal agenda' is that it has sapped too much of the political energy and lessened attention on the priority of unemployment. Issues like contraception, abortion and divorce Blaney says 'are important to some people, to sectional groups and so on, but the 300,000 people unemployed are the priority'. He adds that 'there were "X" cases years ago and nobody paid any attention. There's nothing new happening today that didn't happen before. This is one of the things you learn as you go through life. There's nothing new under the sun – on the social front or otherwise.' On the general economic situation, however, Blaney admits that 'unemployment has been and will continue to be the absolute crisis in society'.

— 9 —
Epilogue

When Neil Blaney was dismissed from Cabinet in May 1970 because of his alleged involvement in the importation of arms, he was entering what should have been his prime political years. Thirteen years a Government Minister when the Arms Crisis broke, it seemed as the 1970s beckoned that Blaney's position in Fianna Fáil and national politics was well secure. If Neil Blaney had put his head down during the 1969-70 period, at the very least his political career at the top would probably have continued for many more years. Gerry Jones, who was close to Blaney throughout this period, believes that 'one could say that in the circumstances which prevailed at that time that he wasn't a good politician'. Regardless of the opinions of his views on Northern Ireland, Neil Blaney did remain true to his convictions and because of this he tore his political career apart.

'In the political storm that blew up in the Republic over the events in Northern Ireland, Blaney was the sufferer, there's no question about that.' So says Brian Lenihan who has been a member of the Oireachtas with Blaney for over thirty years and is in probably one of the best positions to reflect on Blaney's political career to date. He says of Blaney, 'He's a natural politician, he was a natural Minister and he would have made a natural Taoiseach. I think he would have run the country well. But then the Northern crisis came up, it torpedoed him and the Fianna Fáil party. It was a little like one of those Greek tragedies'.

In his book on the Arms Trial, *Through the Bridewell Gate*, Tom Mac Intyre wrote of Blaney, 'He whom London, right or wrong, saw as the South's Ian Paisley. Chunky Donegal man, face long as a Lurgan spade, desolation and humour there – the classic Irish mix, the humour losing though, and likely to continue losing with the years. A born politician, and not without charm as a man. Donegal had given him that as well as the grit. His relationship with Donegal, indeed, gave you the measure of him: they would wash Blaney's feet for him in Donegal – if he asked them. That was a mistake he would never make – he read the peasant in himself and in them far too well. The hand-shake, the grin, the lick of charm, that was a rhythm they both knew. It had served so far. Let it stand'.

While Blaney has achieved much over the last twenty years or so, there must be a sense of personal regret that he has spent these prime years on the sidelines. The outbreak of the Northern Troubles most certainly 'torpedoed' Blaney's career, as Lenihan accurately points out. One commentator feels that 'the face like a Lurgan spade, has indeed lost a lot of its humour over these years'. Although Neil Blaney would never admit it, deep down there must be a feeling of 'what might have been'. In 1985 when speculation of his return to Fianna Fáil was at its height, Neil Blaney was asked if he would like to see himself in Cabinet once again. 'That is the presumption of people who support me and their wish and the wish of a great number of people in Fianna Fáil who want this rift to be solved,' Blaney said as he added that he would enjoy running a Department again. Yet it was never to be so.

Neil Blaney would never openly admit that his political talents have been wasted on the sidelines since 1970. Those who say he has contributed little new over the last ten to twenty years are quietly dismissed. Blaney, like any other politician, has his own agenda, of which the ending of partition and the elimination of the socio-economic deprivation of the north-eastern part of this island are the two most prominent items. Over the last two decades Blaney has worked on these political priorities through his membership of both the European and the National Parliaments. Kevin Boland, recognises the important role Blaney has played since his parting with Fianna Fáil in 1972. 'He's the only voice now that can be heard on partition . . . he can't be ignored.' While Boland does not regret his own decision to resign his Dáil seat in 1970, he says that he now recognises the importance of Blaney's actions at that time. 'My responsibility is to hold my seat,' is what Boland says Blaney told him in 1970. 'What he meant by that, and I only realised it afterwards, was that his responsibility was to be able to hold his seat so that he would always be able to put forward his views.'

While Neil Blaney has been able to articulate his views through his membership of the Dáil and the European Parliament, it is obvious that articulating opinions and implementing them are totally different things. Being outside Fianna Fáil has kept Blaney from wielding the all important power of Government. 'In terms of domestic Irish politics he has cut himself off completely in the last twenty-three years and he has had little or no impact over that time,' is the opinion of one former colleague. Maurice Manning, Fine Gael Senator and political academic, is less severe when he says that, 'The Arms Trial and the Northern problems marginalised him and his enormous talent has been sidelined ever since. But sidelined or not he has always been a formidable figure and little has escaped his attention over those past forty-five years.'

Yet, when assessing Neil Blaney's career it would be wrong simply to start with the Arms Crisis dismissal and consider only the events of the last twenty years. Blaney's career must be evaluated over the entire span of his involvement in national political life. It is true that Neil Blaney will be remembered because of his involvement in the Arms Crisis, and while his views on Northern Ireland mark him out, it is again worth repeating that Blaney is not a one-dimensional politician. Neither has his political career been one-dimensional. It is a political career that the majority of members of the Oireachtas would dearly love to experience: a Dáil deputy for forty-five years with thirteen of those years spent as a Government Minister along with two terms as a member of the European Parliament. Added to these would be the legendary by-election campaigns throughout the 1960s and his ability at keeping together his own group of supporters after his expulsion from Fianna Fáil. Against all odds, Blaney has not only secured his position in Donegal, but he has gone on to widen his scope with his membership of the European Parliament.

When Gerry Jones speaks of his friend Neil Blaney, one senses a feeling of great respect. Jones believes that 'Blaney wanted power to achieve an end which was the unification of Ireland'. History will show that Neil Blaney's achievement in this regard will not be recorded as he would have wished. The Arms Affair, rather than being recalled as the defining act in achieving a united Ireland, remains shrouded in ambiguity and controversy. Until the entire story, if it is ever known, emerges then the significance of the affair and the motivations of those involved cannot be adequately recorded. One reliable source believes that, 'Blaney is one of the few who know the whole and true story. He should not fear telling the truth'. These events in 1969-70 most certainly did turn out to be pivotal in the careers of several of the country's major politicians, including Neil Blaney.

Neil Blaney started his political career in Fianna Fáil. According to Gerry Collins, 'Blaney really worked exceptionally hard for the party, it was his whole life, his whole interest and his whole effort. This is really true.' Yet, barring some unexpected event, Neil Blaney is unlikely to end his political days in the party for which both his father and he himself gave so much. As one former colleague in Fianna Fáil says, 'The issue of his return is at this stage academic'. For Neil Blaney this may be true, but it is not so if the Blaney legacy which stretches back to the foundation of Fianna Fáil is to endure after Neil Blaney is gone. An analysis of the outcome of the vote in Donegal North East illustrates that Neil Blaney's vote has slipped in recent times and, although there is no danger to his own seat, the likelihood is that Independent Fianna Fáil will not be strong enough to hold the Blaney seat, even with a Blaney as their candidate. Neil Blaney is far too proud a man to apply for membership of Fianna Fáil, but those who come after him may be less proud. They will not carry the bitter baggage that has soured relations between Fianna Fáil and those supporters of Neil Blaney.

Whatever happens one thing is assured – Neil Blaney has led an extraordinary political career and one that is unlikely to be forgotten. He has most certainly aroused the emotions and feelings of his political contemporaries over the last forty-five years. Of all the things said and written about him Blaney, putting more tobacco into his pipe, merely reclines in his chair and says in his dry Donegal accent, 'I'd be regarded as many, many things, none of which is probably quite true – but all of them might make me up'.

Bibliography

While writing this book I interviewed a number of politicans, political commentators and associates of Neil Blaney. I also consulted a range of national and local newspapers including *The Irish Times, The Irish Press, The Sunday Press* and *The Donegal Democrat.* Use is made of inteviews given by Neil Blaney to various newspapers and magazines including *Hot Press, Hibernia* and *Magill.* The books listed below are among those used as background research.

Boland Kevin, *We won't stand (idly) by,* (Dublin 1971)

Browne Vincent, *The Magill Book of Irish Politics,* Magill Publications, 1981

Downey James, *Them & Us Britain, Ireland & The Northern Question 1969-82,* Ward River Press 1983

Lee J.J., *Ireland 1912-1985,* Cambridge University Press, 1989

O'Connell John, *Doctor John – Crusading Doctor & Politician,* Poolbeg, 1989

O'Malley Padraig, *Biting at the Grave – The Irish Hunger Strikes and the Politics of Despair,* Blackstaff Press, 1990

Mac Intyre Tom, *Through the Bridewell Gate, A Diary of the Dublin Arms Trial,* Faber and Faber, 1971

Sacks Paul, *The Donegal Mafia,* Yale University Press, 1976

Walsh Dick, *The Party: Inside Fianna Fáil,* Gill and Macmillan, 1986

Index